FRIENDS

VOICES ON THE GIFT OF COMPANIONSHIP

AMY LOU JENKINS   LEAH ANGSTMAN

LAURA AUSTIN   ELAN BARNEHAMA

MARA BUCK   TERRI ELDERS   TAK ERZINGER

NATALIE ESAREY   JANET GARBER

KATHLEEN GERARD   PAT HALE

MYLES HOPPER   RICH H. KENNEY, JR

NANCY LONDON   STEVE LUEBKE

LEE MELAHN   JULIA ANNE MILLER

JOANNE PASSET   ADRIENNE PINE

BETSY ROBINSON   PATTY SOMLO

CHRIS WIEWIORA   TAMRA WILSON   P.F. WITTE

PRAISE FOR 'FRIENDS'

The diverse voices and experiences of these writers is nicely juxtaposed in a heartwarming collection that is invitingly filled with revealing personal messages: *"...the death of my best friend isn't the topic. I'm here to celebrate her life and to share the life she so graciously shared with me—the life that helped to save me. We became best friends in what felt like an instant. I loved her with my whole heart, and I know full well that she loved me with all of hers. We understood each other in a way no one else could. We were both sick. Hers was physical, and mine, mental, but we were both ill."*

As the stories evolve, readers will relish the personal tones, touches, and explorations that consider the nature of friendship, its gifts and resiliency, and its lasting impact on all.

Most of all, this inspirational read captures those often-fleeting moments of friendship that change and influence lives, even years later: *"I can't remember saying goodbye or feeling bad about leaving Carla or even missing her. In fact, I can't remember which of us left Germany first. I recollect that we didn't keep in touch. I don't have a clue what happened to Carla, and writing this, I realize I've never wondered about it before."*

Perhaps that's the single most special strength of this series of diary-like descriptions of special relationships remembered—the ability to celebrate their ongoing impact on lives even after they have long passed.

Readers looking for personal vignettes about friendship will find *Friends: Voices On The Gift Of Companionship* an outstanding key to understanding how relationships evolve, change, pass, and often come full circle to become even more valued as the years go by.

—D. Donovan, Sr. Reviewer, Midwest Book Review

We fill our homes with posters, pillows, and trinkets scrawled with inspirational phrases celebrating the bonds of love that bind us to those closest to us. "Friends Forever," like "Happily Ever After," is an ultimate goal in a personal connection. Our epithets highlight the joy and beauty of such a close bond, dusting it in gold and adding a starlight filter just for good measure.

What we choose to ignore most of the time is that friendship, like any interpersonal connection, is a lot of hard work. It doesn't always last. And even when it does, it's almost certainly not the gilded good time that our slogans would suggest.

Friends: Voices on the Gift of Companionship will take you through the full spectrum of what it means to call someone "friend." The authors who contributed to this collection aren't here to give you the warm-and-fuzzies. These essays are an open, honest, and often raw look at what it means to call someone a friend.

Loss, envy, and love are the common threads that run throughout *Friends*. Some authors grapple with how to love someone even as they both envy and pity them. Others, with maintaining love and legacy even after saying goodbye to a life well-lived. But the beautiful thing about each chapter is that every story is unique. Although these themes unite the authors, vivid details of unique personalities and settings make each chapter its own experience.

Friends: Voices on the Gift of Companionship isn't the book on coffee table your meant to be skimmed and smiled at. Friends is the book on your nightstand that you reach for when you need to feel connected to humanity.   —Skye McDonald author of the Anti-Belle series

---

The authors in this anthology come from a wide range of backgrounds, and share their stories of friendship with convincing, if often difficult, passages. Their collective friends have been challenged by alternate lifestyles, alcohol, abuse, abandonment, relationship demise, cancer, and suicide...yielding the lesson to be good to our friends while we can. If it is too late to offer comfort or encouragement, we may still regard the gifts of shared histories as nourishment to sustain us.   —Carol Barrett, Ph.D. Coordinator, Creative Writing Certificate Program, Union Institute & University; author of *Calling in the Bones* (poems) and *Pansies* (nonfiction.)

The voices in this fascinating collection of essays on friendship come through loud and clear with important and insightful messages we all need to hear. During the course of our lives, we encounter many people who we interact and connect with, in whatever capacity. There are some people we relate to more than others, and perhaps what we see in these same people are some traces of ourselves. As much as I enjoyed reading the various essays, I also appreciated that the stories were organized into various categories, such as, "The Helpers," and "Unspoken," amongst other important groupings, to help readers distinguish between and better understand the different types of friendships we cultivate.

There are as many stories of friendships as there are types of friendships, as each author so eloquently describes in his or her story. Just as quickly as people appear in our lives, they often disappear, leaving us bereft and bewildered about what became of our friendships. Of course, there is the other side of the coin, with authors sharing tales of enduring friendships that withstand the weathering of the passage of time. There are also tales of people discovering that they now feel close to someone who they least expected to be called their friend. However long our friendships last or not, the people we call, or at one time called, friends, each makes a definite impact on us in their own unique ways.

This is a must-read for anyone who has ever had or been a friend to someone else!

A thoroughly enjoyable and heartfelt read! This is an invaluable book for anyone seeking insight and comprehension of the convoluted and often misunderstood road we travel known as friendship. A definite 5-star rating!

—International Review of Books

978-1-945378-08-9   Paperback

978-1-945378-09-6   Hardcover

Friends:
Voices on the Gift of Companionship
by Amy Lou Jenkins et al
1. Literary Collections/Essays 2. Biography & Autobiography/Personal
Memoirs 3. Family and Relationships 4. Friendship

For all who honor us with the gift of friendship for a day, for a season, or for a lifetime. Thank you dear friend.

CONTENTS

PART VIII
STILL TOGETHER

INTRODUCTION

If someone gave you this book, they probably cherish you.

You may imagine that a book of friend-stories could read as a collection of tributes about great friends, and this book does celebrate pals and companions who make our lives richer. I wondered if we'd hear from writers who had dozens of decades-long friendships and that they would make me consider myself a failure as a friend—a sad-sack, with only a handful of pals scattered across the country. Yet, as the submissions arrived for this collection, some patterns emerged that told tales of beautiful entanglements. Everything isn't always rosy in a deep friendship, and these stories speak to the complexity of that truth. Most relationships end; that doesn't make them a failure or have to diminish their joys. While best and bestish friends, who arrive in our youth and remain bonded to us through old age, do enrich our days, other kinds of buddies and companions, who weave in and out of our days and years, also scaffold our lives. They are all important.

***

When my youngest, my son Dylan, was six, I escaped my suburban life for a girls' weekend with my best friend, Ginny. She had moved to Ft. Lauderdale. (You will read more about her in Chapter 24) and undergone some radical changes. The plan: I'd fly in from Milwaukee; then, we'd drive to Key West. I'd arrange some activities in the upper and middle Keys, and she'd take charge in Key West.

I'd missed my friend, who had moved away five years before. While I'd become more reserved since having another baby and settling into a more domestic and suburban life, she'd gone wild. I went back to grad school while she'd shopped for services at tattoo and piercing parlors. I worked in nursing administration, and she'd become a traveling nurse and nudist. My weekends—filled with school activities, sports, and motherly duties—hers busy with outings to clothing-optional beaches and clothing-optional dates. My husband probably worried a bit as he drove me to the airport. I, on the other hand, was cheery and chatty in anticipation of a brief retreat with my friend, until a radio news report about the Boy Scouts shattered my jovial mood.

I'd recently become the Cub Scout den leader for Dylan and his friends. I loved them, and the promise of sharing my love of the natural world with them. They were now old enough for hikes, fishing, birding, and fun outdoor excitements that I never got to explore in my stupid Brownie troop, where we made party favors and embroidered a turkey placemat that I accidentally sewed to my skirt.

The car radio announced that The Boy Scouts of America officially prohibited gay leaders and members. The BSA would eventually soften, then reverse their stance, and then things would get even more complicated when tales of abuse against boys emerged. Yet, at that time, my anxiety about supporting and participating in a homophobic group led me to believe that I really had to quit Scouting. I mourned giving up time with my only son and his friends and nurturing their love for the outdoors. How could I disappoint the boys when they rightly didn't give two hoots about labels like gay or straight? But I felt that I must resign.

I boarded the plane with angst, which receded into the background by the time Ginny and I rented a convertible and began driving through the Keys, marveling at those bright blue skies, and long ocean bridges. We stopped at Annie's Beach for a picnic, swam with the dolphins at the research center on Grassy Key, and watched Green Bay win at the self-proclaimed southernmost Packers bar. Then, we drove on to Key West.

Ginny took charge and drove us straight to a clothing-optional gay resort, describing the hotel as we arrived and adding, "After check-in, there's a party."

Though I was freaked out internally, I tried to act nonchalant and asked some questions: "Will people be nude at this party?"

"Probably," she answered.

"Will you be nude?"

"Maybe."

"Will you be okay with the fact that I will remain fully clothed?"

"Do whatever feels comfortable."

Comfortable? Impossible.

The party room had a bar, a DJ, and long tables draped in white paper tablecloths. It looked sort of like a church basement wedding reception, except a few people were nude. Others had cut-outs in their clothing with bits, generally not for public viewing, exposed. This seemed like just the kind of thing the Boy Scouts of America would worry about. I was a nurse, so nakedness itself didn't bother me per se, but the out-of-place nudity did evoke unease.

We ordered gin and tonics and found seats. Immediately, we met three friendly guys who introduced themselves as part of a loving, polyamorous relationship. Soon Ginny and the guys revealed tattoos to each other. Clothes were pulled aside like curtains to expose more tattoos and piercings that I tried not to look at. Instead, I inspected the ice in my gin and tonic. One of the guys complimented Ginny on her yellow halter dress; she asked him if he'd like to try it on. In a quick over-the-head sweep, off came the dress. Dropping it over his head, the guy began to twirl, and off to the dance-floor they went.

One of the trio stayed behind with me. I don't recall his name, but I do remember his compassion as he sensed my discomfort. He looked shy of 30, with a well-groomed dark beard and bright green eyes. "Are you two a couple?" he asked.

I explained my heterosexual, monogamous marriage and my long-term relationship with my wild best friend. We quickly fell into a conversational closeness. He shared about his loves and about his mother, who was unhappy, perhaps tortured because of his sexuality. He seemed sweet, dedicated to trying to help me feel at ease. He shared that he was a middle-school teacher. Eventually, I told him about my Cub Scout dilemma. He asked me to tell him about the boys. I explained:

Dylan's spray of freckles dances across his nose and cheeks as he smiles and chatters. He's not self-conscious about how much he loves people. He compliments almost everyone, telling strangers they have nice shoes and old ladies they have great purple hair. He gives away his school supplies to kids who don't have any paste or tape or crayons.

Omar can't say his R's but can do math in his head faster than most adults, and he loves to learn about trees and rocks.

Ralph's parents died, so he lives with his uncle. I don't think his aunt likes him. He's sad and looks down at his feet most of the time, but he seems to like the meetings and hangs close to me.

I'm sure I must have continued on about the boys and about my concerns at being part of an institution of homophobia.

My new friend told me that he was an awkward, weird kid, but he felt like he fit in at Scouts, saying a lot of oddballs end up in Scouts, and it's a place where they can mix to some extent with the more athletic and socially viable sorts. And these words I do remember specifically: he told me, "Don't quit. Stay as their leader. You'll make a difference. They need you." By the end of the night, we were hugging and chatting like reunited sorority sisters, yet we were companions for only one evening.

When I got home, I wrote a letter to the BSA and formally objected to their policy of rejecting and denouncing all homosexuals. I didn't quit. I stayed with those boys from Tiger Scouts, Cub Scouts, and through Webelos. I still know most of these men, now graduated from college, starting careers, and getting married. I watch their lives progress on Facebook. They are good men.

Dylan and I went on to spend time outdoors together, even after Scouting, and those times were the subject of my first book, *Every Natural Fact: Five Seasons of Open-Air Parenting.*

I would have never received credible absolution to stay in Scouting if I hadn't followed my wild friend to a scary place to meet a beautiful, pierced, tattooed, gay teacher in a loving polyamorous relationship, who offered himself as companion to me for an evening, and who gave me great advice.

The implicit advice from the stories that follow seem to broaden our definition of successful friendships. We cherish our long-term friends. And perhaps those friends we grew apart from or those friendships that only lasted a short time served an essential role for a season. And for those people in long-term friendships, know that you are fortunate.

Civilizations as far back as the Greeks and Romans understood the value of buddies and gave thanks to the goddess of friendship and affection, Philotes. When those ancients offered thanks to her, they personified a deep love for their companions, who gave witness to and enriched their lives. Philotes may not hear many prayers directed her way these days, but whomever collects those present-day expressions of gratitude, let's hope that our friends are among those notified.

In these stories, many of the authors changed the names and some of the identifiers for confidentiality and respect, but they left the rawness and honesty that reside within these explorations of vital relationships. It is my great hope that as you read these stories, you will understand how important your friendship has been to others. I also wish that these personal narratives will expand your sense of gratitude for every friend who has and who will come your way.

—Amy Lou Jenkins

PART I

THE HELPERS

This is my wish for you: comfort on difficult days, smiles when sadness intrudes, rainbows to follow the clouds, laughter to kiss your lips, sunsets to warm your heart, hugs when spirits sag, beauty for your eyes to see, friendships to brighten your being, faith so that you can believe, confidence for when you doubt, courage to know yourself, patience to accept the truth, love to complete your life.

—Ralph Waldo Emerson

1

CAROLE'S PROJECTS

JOANNE PASSET

As the plane descends over Los Angeles, I stare at a mosaic of rust-colored tile roofs and swimming pools and wonder if it's too late to change my mind, to turn down the job, and to return to Indiana and my failed marriage. It's 1988, the year I begin again. I move through my anxiety toward something new.

Once outside the terminal, I'm mesmerized by palm trees silhouetted against a brilliant blue sky until honking cars and exhaust fumes interrupt my reverie. "Can you take me to UCLA?" I ask a Super Shuttle driver, and within minutes, he's whisking me onto the 405 toward Westwood and the university subsidized apartment I've rented sight unseen. I've moved to Los Angeles without a car because I've never enjoyed driving and naively expect this sprawling metropolis to have good public transportation.

For a few days, I resemble a cat in a new house, going out and back from my apartment to a nearby taco stand, a grocery, and a movie theater. School doesn't start until late September, but when Monday arrives, I walk across campus, past Ackerman Union, and up the hill to Powell Library, home of the Graduate School of Library and Information Science, where I'll be teaching. The building is quiet, but in the office, I find a woman, in her early fifties, making copies. She wears a flowing calf-length skirt, and her salt and pepper hair hangs in a ponytail from the crown of her head. My farmer father would have called her stout, meaning it as a compliment. "Good morning!" She collects pages from the machine. "What a beautiful day!"

I nod, trying to remember if I met her during my interview.

"I'm Carole," she offers. "We've been expecting you! Wait here; I'll get your office key."

I spot the nameplate on her desk and remember—she's the administrative secretary who fielded my endless questions about finding a place.

"When did you arrive? Are you settled into your new apartment?" She peppers me with questions as I follow her to an office door bearing my married name. Apologetic, I point to the nameplate and mention I returned to my maiden name after the divorce. "No worries." She throws her arms around me in a quick hug, then slips it from the frame. "I'll have a new one for you before you can say Jack Robinson."

In the weeks before fall quarter begins, most faculty work at home, but campus offers an escape from the solitary confinement of my apartment. My files organized and courses prepped, I spend hours on the patio of UCLA's Kerckhoff Coffee House trying to write while people around me discuss politics, the latest movies, and noise pollution. Their caffeinated energy keeps loneliness at bay.

Weekends, however, are a different matter. From late Friday afternoon until Monday morning, my only interactions are with the postal carrier, movie ticket salesperson, or grocery store clerk. Initially, I relish the opportunity to read entire books in one sitting and spend hours writing journal entries. But evenings are long, and I find myself pondering what went wrong with my happily-ever-after. When doubts threaten to overwhelm me, I buy spumoni and eat from the carton until it's empty.

"How was your weekend?" Carole asks one Monday.

"Fine." I assume she's making polite conversation, but then realize she's waiting for me to elaborate. "Actually, I had another nonverbal weekend."

"What? We can't have that." She thinks for a few seconds. "You must still need things for your apartment. Why don't I take you shopping Saturday, and if there's time, we'll stop afterward to see LACMA's new Pavilion for Japanese Art. I'll drive!"

I hesitate, wondering if I should be socializing with office staff. But to be honest, the faculty intimidate me with their polysyllabic vocabularies and constant namedropping. In their presence, I feel like an imposter. "I'd love an outing," I tell Carole, who whoops with delight.

On Saturday morning, I'm waiting in front of my apartment when a faded blue Chevy slows to a stop. As I step back, the driver cranks down the passenger window, and a cheerful voice calls, "Jo-ANNE!" Carole's grinning wide, a feather tucked in her hair. I wrench open the door and survey the cracked blue vinyl upholstery, sagging roof liner, and a back seat overflowing with clothing and kitchen wares.

"People call this my rolling wardrobe," Carole laughs as we ease into traffic for the drive to her favorite bakery. "I collect items for Santana and Adam at the pueblo." I have no idea who she's talking about, but don't ask because I want her to focus on driving.

Vienna Pastry is crowded, its glass cases filled with buttery Danishes, apple strudel, and cookies. "You have to try the fruit tarts," Carole exclaims. As we wait in line to pay, she greets employees by first name, asks if the cashier's daughter has had her baby yet, and offers advice to a customer with an ailing cat. I shift back and forth, admiring her effortless interactions with people.

Fortified by coffee and lemon-raspberry tarts, we continue on our way. "Wertz Brothers has the best used furniture," Carole informs me as she maneuvers into a tight parking space. The store lives up to her pronouncement. In the end, I purchase a drop-leaf table and four chairs, but when the clerk offers to deliver them for a fee, Carole intervenes. "No thanks! We'll take them ourselves." Returning to the parking lot, she digs through her back seat for a length of rope, then persuades a Wertz employee to tie my table and chairs to the Chevy's roof.

"Would you like to go anywhere else?" Carole asks as we turn onto Santa Monica Boulevard. Shaking my head, I study the dashboard to avoid accidental eye contact with passing drivers. Despite my protests, Carole turns into Pier One and convinces me to buy a wicker settee, which we add to her rooftop. We decide to visit the museum another day.

The following weekend, with Carole's encouragement, I convince a visiting faculty member to accompany me on an outing. We take a bus downtown and disembark on Spring Street, near the Greyhound Bus station. A flower market catches our attention, and when we return to the street, we're each cradling a Christmas cactus. Our plan is to walk to Little Tokyo, but we misread the map and find ourselves in Skid Row. Swarms of young men mill about, and gaunt skeletons sleep in doorways and under pieces of cardboard. "Walk with a purpose," my colleague advises me as we step over used needles, broken beer bottles, and trash. Once we reach our destination, we collapse in relief.

"Until you're familiar with the city," Carole advises upon learning about our excursion, "I'll show you around." I'm not used to people befriending me like this, and I wonder why she cares. Then I realize, I'm not her only project. She's advising a perplexed bachelor about women, babysitting for a single Mom, and counseling co-workers about diet and exercise. She seems to have solutions for everyone.

In the coming weeks, Carole fills my calendar with exhibit openings at the Getty, excursions to fabric stores, and sales at Trader Joes. "How can I ever repay you?" I fret after one of our outings. "You won't," she says without batting an eye. "I do things because I enjoy them, and you honor me by being a gracious recipient. One day, you'll be in a position to do the same for others."

In November, Carole tells me she's holding a sewing circle at her apartment. "You should come! You don't have to sew; just bring something to do. You'll like the people!" Arriving early, I climb the steps to her one-bedroom, rent-controlled apartment. Every surface is covered. Stacks of books, magazines, and newspapers join colorful serapes and Mexican pottery in welcoming visitors into her living room. *Peanuts* cartoons, children's drawings, photos of friends, and birthday cards decorate the refrigerator in Carole's galley-style kitchen. Cans of cat food, tins of cookie cutters, and old Kleenex boxes stuffed with coupons and recipes from the *L.A. Times* cover her table. "You should try this recipe for granola," Carole says, pressing it into my hand. "It calls for flaxseed!"

She steps onto a plant-filled patio. "Let me introduce you to Walks-a-Lot, Ralphie, Gertrude, Blackie, and Turtle," she beams, motioning to five cats dozing in the late-afternoon sun. I find myself wondering where she keeps their litter boxes.

When other guests arrive, Carole pushes books and papers aside and urges us to sit on her daybed, plastic lawn chairs, and pillows piled on the floor. As we settle into companionable chatter, I marvel at her ability to create community from such a diverse array of individuals, and I'm grateful I entered her orbit.

Carole is on the patio, cutting slips for one of the guests, when a woman near me points to a pottery book on the coffee table. "When I first met Carole, she was a different person—anxious, timid, and always looking for a missing piece of herself."

I nod, finding this hard to picture.

"Then, in the early seventies, she took a pottery workshop at Idyllwild and met Santana and Adam Martinez, the famous San Ildefonso Pueblo potters. You've heard of them?"

I shake my head: yes.

"Afterward, Carole started corresponding with Santana, and the next thing we knew, she was visiting New Mexico. It was the first of many trips, and each time, she collected a carload of art supplies, clothing, and more for people at the Pueblo."

I nod again, remembering the rolling wardrobe.

"Something happened there because Carole came back changed—serene, more content, and above all, able to care for others without losing herself. She said the place and its people, especially Santana, had indescribably touched her. When we pressed for more, she said they had taught her about gratitude and community."

I'm mulling this over when one of the guests cries, "Carole!" and points to the kitchen. Following her finger, I see a cat on the counter, licking the crust of an apple pie.

"Shoo!" Carole hurries into the kitchen, admonishing the cat as it jumps to the floor with a thud. *So much for pie*, I think, but I'm mistaken. Carole flicks grains of sugar from the pie's crust and sets the oven to broil. "That'll take care of the germs. Now, who wants pie *a la mode*?"

In the coming months, Carole introduces me to countless international films and restaurants. On weekends, we purchase lemons and oranges at neighborhood farmers' markets, visit world-class museums, and walk through a flea market held at the Rose Bowl. We join a Burned Books Brigade to help the Los Angeles Public Library in the aftermath of its devastating fire. Emboldened by her adventurousness, I take a solo trip to the Hollywood Bowl and outings to Venice Beach. I exchange my glasses for contacts and lose weight. Life is good.

In the spring of my second year at UCLA, I'm offered a faculty position at Indiana University. I debate whether to remain in the City of Angels or return to the land of meateaters, cheesy casseroles, and Jell-O. I'm energized by L.A.'s sunshine, spontaneity, and my encounters with people from all over the world. On the other hand, I'd be near my elderly parents, and I'm steeped in a strong sense of duty to family. After much deliberation, I accept the job, hoping I can preserve my changed sense of self.

Returning to the Midwest is like putting on a familiar garment, only to find it no longer fits. My colleagues define themselves by their workloads, competing to see who stayed up the latest grading papers, who has the most students, and who's teaching summer school. I resolve not to feel guilty if I go to a movie or take a weekend excursion but fail miserably.

By late October, when chilly rains strip trees of their colorful coats, I'm plagued by doubts. Why did I leave California? Will I ever feel at home here? How can I preserve my L.A. outlook on life? I don't want to worry my parents, and I'm afraid to reveal weakness to new colleagues, so I pour out my concerns in a letter to Carole, the only person I know who won't judge me.

A few days later, I arrive home from work to find one of her care packages, a tin filled with apricot balls rolled in powdered sugar, homemade cranberry-almond biscotti, and packets of Good Earth tea. She also sends a book, *Two Old Women*. Settling down with a cup of tea, I read the story of two elderly Eskimos left by their tribe to die, and I wonder why Carole chose it for me. Then it becomes obvious: like these women, I'm stronger than I think, and the path to happiness lies within myself.

In the coming weeks, I settle into the rhythm of my new position. I join a book group, start a knitting circle, and take a creative writing class. Life is better, yet when semester break arrives, and winter settles over the Midwest, I book a flight to L.A. "You can sleep on my daybed," Carole announces when I phone with news of my upcoming visit.

Greeting me at the airport with a bear hug, Carole cheerfully outlines the week's activities— —yoga, yoga, and more yoga. "Yoga Works was running a special, so I bought you a guest membership! It's much cheaper than paying per session while you're here."

"But I didn't bring yoga clothes." I should have known she would take me to one of her favorite activities.

"Not a problem," Carole declares, driving me to Goodwill, where she rummages through tubs of exercise clothing and selects a fuchsia leotard and purple tights. "These are your colors," she grins, pushing me toward the cashier.

That afternoon, I stuff my workout costume in a plastic bag and wait for Carole to emerge from her bedroom.

"Why aren't you dressed for yoga?"

"I thought I'd change there."

Carole shakes her head, and I know it's useless to resist.

Giving the driver a cheery hello, Carole seems to think nothing of us boarding a Santa Monica bus in leotards and tights, yoga mats slung over our shoulders. When we arrive at a chic Montana Avenue studio, filled with aspiring actresses and screenwriters, I take my mat to a corner spot while she strikes up a conversation with a young woman at the front of the room. I'm stretching when I hear, "Jo-ANNE." Looking up, I see Carole motion for me to join her. Everyone around us wears calming shades of sage green, powder blue, or black, and I want to sink through the floor. As we settle into our practice, it takes me longer than usual to center myself.

The next day, we're about to leave for a movie when it starts to rain. "No worries!" Carole announces, rooting through her closet until she finds two bright yellow rain slickers. Only after I put it on do I see the big "War is NOT the Answer" bumper sticker plastered across the front. "I wore it to a protest at the Federal Building last month," Carole explains as we walk to the bus stop. I wonder what my life would be like if I could be as comfortable in my skin as Carole, if I no longer spent time worrying about what people think of my purple leotard, yellow rain slicker, divorce, weight, and all the other things Midwesterners chew over like a cow does its cud.

The week flies by, and the evening before my departure, Carole shoos me to the patio to enjoy late afternoon sunshine while she prepares beef stew in a cast-iron kettle. Hummingbirds dart back and forth among hanging baskets as we eat on faded plastic chairs. Below us, in the alley, a woman tosses a large box into the dumpster. "You never know what you'll find," Carole says, tearing down the stairs and returning a few minutes later with a Lava Lamp. We plug it in and sit for the remainder of the evening, enthralled by dancing blue bubbles.

The next morning, Carole tucks the leotard and tights into my suitcase. "You'll need these in Indiana!" She tries to send the Lava Lamp too, but it's too heavy.

For the next eighteen years, Carole is my most faithful correspondent. Her letters, signed, "Love and hugs, Carole," alternate with packages of used books about cooking, art, needlework, and pioneering women. I write about my classes, research, and parents while she shares stories of mourning dove eggs hatching on her patio, recipes, and reviews of art exhibits and foreign films she knows I'd enjoy. Each letter is a gift, grounding me in things that matter, helping me achieve balance. Before long, she's also corresponding with my elderly mother, sending her books and homemade biscotti that Mom mistakes for dog biscuits.

Three years after Carole's retirement, she's diagnosed with cancer. In her typical fashion, she bakes cookies for her chemotherapy nurses and learns the life stories of other patients. Chemo renders her bald, and I knit her a purple cap, which she wears under a red straw hat. When she can no longer navigate the steps to her home, Carole moves to a garden apartment, and an array of friends provide round-the-clock care and companionship until she draws her last breath. I take the news hard because I thought there'd be one more visit, one more yoga class, one more letter. Instead, I travel to Los Angeles for her memorial service in June 2008.

A former UCLA colleague meets my plane, and after a short drive, we pull into a busy strip mall off Santa Monica

Boulevard. A gust of cool air washes over me as we step inside Carole's favorite restaurant, Monte Alban. I join the others at a long row of tables placed end-to-end and marvel at the range of Carole's network of friends: deans and secretaries, lawyers and hippies, professors and yoga practitioners, nurses, and neighbors. Our ages range from three to eighty, and we're many colors and ethnicities. Even though some of us have never met, there's a sense of connection.

"Carole loved the mole here," a woman to my right announces. She beckons to a waitress, who brings a platter topped with colorful melamine bowls filled with samples of red, brown, green, black, and yellow mole. "Carole loved Oaxacan food and was on a one-woman campaign to ensure small family-run businesses survived. She'd come here for lunch, and if someone stopped by her apartment later the same day and suggested dining out, she'd say, "Let's go to Monte Alban!"

"That's why we're here," her attorney explains. "Carole didn't want a traditional memorial service. Instead, she asked me to use money from her estate, so you could gather together at one of her favorite places." Glasses clink as we toast our friend.

When our bellies are filled with enchiladas, tacos, fajitas, burritos, and mole, a secretary rises at the other end of the table. "How many of you were recipients of Carole's 'should' lectures? "There were so many," she laughs. "I started numbering them. My favorite was number twenty-eight, 'you should retire.'"

When our laughter subsides, the Greek man who lived next door to Carole remembers her love of yoga. "As a retirement gift to herself, she bought a lifetime membership to Yoga Works, her one extravagance in an otherwise frugal existence. How many of you are here because Carole thought you should do yoga?" I raise my hand, along with many others. "That was 'should' lecture number one," he chuckles.

A woman Carole met at a farmer's market speaks next. "We all know how much she loved discovering treasures at thrift stores—pieces of silver, pewter, postcards, and especially books." Laughter fills the room. "She may have collected stuff, but we were her most treasured collection. She took good care of us and never threw anyone away." Lucy holds both hands palm up, motioning to her right and left. "We are the living proof."

Carole's obituary in the *L.A. Times* described her as "a woman of grace and indomitable spirit" whose simple life enlightened others. I'm grateful to be one of her beneficiaries. Because of Carole, I take time to watch cats washing their faces and bees sipping nectar from sunflowers. I plant an herb garden each spring and eat granola often, but I still haven't developed a taste for flaxseed. I try to be a gracious recipient of gifts and a cheerful giver. At Christmastime, I use Carole's recipes to bake biscotti for friends and knit warm hats, mittens, and scarves for the homeless. I host international students and tutor adult learners at my local library. My bookshelves overflow with eclectic titles. I find peace in practicing yoga, and I often wear purple, turquoise, and fuchsia. I'm no longer Carole's project. Thanks to her, I have many projects of my own.

2

WHAT A BEST FRIEND DOES

RICH H. KENNEY, JR.

It was in late May that I hit my first Little League home run off Wally Sanders, the All-Star fire-baller for Hunt's Potato Chips, at Watson Park in Braintree, Massachusetts. For nearly six decades, May has been a special month for me. And yet, over the years, the reasons for its significance have changed.

As I watched it sail over the centerfield scoreboard, I couldn't believe that I was the one who hit it. For years, when I replayed that moment in my head, I saw the ball exploding off my bat, the ball soaring, and my Penguin A.C. teammates swarming me at home plate.

Well into my thirties and forties, I could still feel the exhilaration of that swing, the elation of knowing that I hit one out—off one of the best pitchers in the league.

At family gatherings, my mother would recall how she spilled coffee on her lap as she watched the ball arc its way out of the park. My uncle would tell me how he was standing at the refreshment stand and how he turned just in the nick of time to witness the launch. Their accounts were always the boosts I seemed to need at the time.

There were a few years when I forgot about the big hit, when the quiet anniversaries were overshadowed by illness, deadlines, or the stress of some job. There were years when I wondered to myself, what's the big deal, anyway? What's with this silly commemoration?

Not too long ago, I came across a photo of an old buddy. Jerry DeCoste was my best friend back in the '50s and early '60s. He was a slick-fielding, left-handed first baseman. We used to ride our bikes to Mutzenard's Variety, where we ate orange Popsicles. He was the neighborhood kid I played catch with for countless hours.

Jerry also played for Hunt's Potato Chips and was the first person I saw as I rounded first base after I hit the home run. There he was, standing with his glove on his hip behind the bag near the foul line.

He didn't say anything. Instead, he grinned, and awkwardly nodded his head in acknowledgement. We were fierce competitors, but, more importantly, we were best friends.

I didn't realize it until recently, but after all these years, the thing I cherish most about that slow-motion moment was the split-second when our eyes met on that dusty infield at

Watson Park. What I saw in his eyes told me what had just happened was a big deal.

That's what a best friend does. That's what Jerry DeCoste did for me one day in late May, 1962.

Previously published in the Patriot Ledger, Quincy, MA, May 19, 2019.

3

A RANDOM ACT

NATALIE ESAREY

I was a freshman in high school, a mere fifteen years old. It's funny because when you are fifteen, and it feels like the weight of the world is on your shoulders, you think that your current struggles are your entire identity. I was no exception. My problems were smaller than some and bigger than others. But they were far too much for me to handle on my own.

I was depressed and undiagnosed. I thought it was all in my head, and even if I believed for a second that my pain was real or valid, the belief vanished when I could not come up with an explanation as to why I was suffering. But that is the thing about depression; it does not always come with a warning or an explanation. No, it just comes: unannounced, unwelcome, and out of nowhere.

My spiraling depression, along with my crumbling self-worth, led me to begin self-harming. The self-harm may have stemmed from the depression, but it seemed to come from a whole different demon: an abusive, manipulative, and even more wicked demon than my depression. I was a little girl carrying a purse that should have been filled with candy and makeup, yet the contents included hidden razor blades placed strategically amongst miscellaneous items used to cover up my biggest secret.

From the moment I used that razor blade for the first time, I swear to you, a certain pain that I had been hiding inside came seeping out. The self-harm took on way more meaning than I ever planned for it to. I had heard that cutting allowed you to release pain, to feel better, and it did —for an instant. But then came an overwhelming sense of worthlessness and this idea that I deserved to not only feel emotional pain but to endure my self-inflicted physical abuse as well. This feeling of consuming worthlessness, and the addition it fueled sent me spiraling, hard and fast. Before I knew it, I was not only using my razor blades every day, multiple times a day, but also etching words into my skin. The words labeled identities like "worthless," "bitch," and "fat." Suffocating sadness plagued me, and worst of all, I felt alone.

I thought no one noticed my pain. Or perhaps they noticed—and they didn't care.

But I was wrong. I was so wrong.

One day, after the bell rang at school, I went to my desk to collect my things. As I went to close my assignment book, I noticed two notes. One read, "you're beautiful," the other, "If those scars aren't really from a cat, call me," with a number I didn't recognize attached.

I was dumbfounded. I was both terrified and relieved that someone had noticed. After school, I whipped out my phone and dialed the number as fast as I could. It rang several times and then sent me to the voicemail. And then I heard it—heard the name of the girl who would soon become my best friend—and eventually, my angel.

You see, this lovely girl who left me a note was sick. She had a terminal illness called mitochondrial disease. It's a disease that attacks every system in the body one by one until it eventually strips you from your life altogether. But the death of my best friend isn't the topic. I'm here to celebrate her life and to share the life she so graciously shared with me—the life that helped to save me.

We became best friends in what felt like an instant. I loved her with my whole heart, and I know full well that she loved me with all of hers. We understood each other in a way no one else could. We were both sick. Hers was physical, and mine, mental, but we were both ill. And when you're so sick and so young, people stray from you. Not because they are bad people, but because it is especially hard to watch a young person you love fade away.

Fast forward two years, and we both had grown sicker yet closer to each other. She was no longer in school. She was now on hospice and in the final weeks of her life. I was wrapped in depression and bound by the chains of the hell that are anorexia and bulimia.

We had both lost so much, so many friends, so many experiences, and so much life. But we never lost each other. And that alone was a reason to keep breathing

I had recently started going to therapy. I had confessed

to my mom about my eating disorder and was starting to get help. It was not my idea, though. It was my best friend's. At the time, I did not want to live for me anymore. But I loved her so much that I decided to keep living for her.

Two weeks before she took her final breath, we were lying in her bed. After some lighthearted talks and gut-wrenching giggles, the room fell silent. And then I looked at her. And I made a promise: I promised her that I would not just continue therapy while she was alive, but that I would continue to fight when she was gone.

Her illness may have been terminal; mine did not have to be. So, I promised with my whole heart that I would beat mine, and it would be our victory to share. We both burst into tears and hugged each other for what we both knew would be the last time.

Fast forward three more years, and guess what? I am still here. Even better, I'm not just here merely existing, I am here alive, well, and happy. I wish I could say it was a smooth ride from the moment I made that promise; it was anything but. I had suicide attempts, treatment centers, and relapses, but you know what I also had? That promise.

I am writing today, not only from a place of peace but also from a place full of hope. I am in solid recovery, and I am beating this thing. The view looking out at all I've over-come is breathtakingly beautiful. But it would be nothing if I did not have anyone to share the victory with.

Thankfully, ever since that day I received the most random act of kindness from a stranger, I have never had to experience anything alone; this is our victory, OUR story of overcoming. We did it. I could not have, and would not want to have, done it without her.

Previously published by *Thought Catalog*, June 19, 2017.

4

ON BOTH HANDS

STEVE LUEBKE

I can't recall the first time I met Dan. It was likely during first grade, but we didn't become good friends until high school, when we played drums together in band. In fifth grade, he taught me how to play the accents in "Wipe Out" by pounding our hands on our desks in math class. When we came in as freshmen, the high school percussion section was dominated by five young women. Oddly, our arrival coincided with a two-year run of almost exclusively male percussionists, and we became the leaders. Band was my favorite class; I'm fairly sure it was Dan's also. So we played together, a lot, in the concert band and wind ensemble, in the marching band (collaboratively composing the drum cadence: I wrote the first half, and he wrote the second), and in the pep band for home basketball games. We played duets at the Solo and Ensemble festival, in which our school participated once a year.

My first memories of him are from grade school: Dan on

the playground, fighting another boy. At my Catholic grade school, a "fight" never involved punches. Rather, it was a physical altercation that resembled wrestling. In this instance, it took the form of Dan hovering above another boy, calmly kneeling on his shoulders so he couldn't escape. Another time, I thoughtlessly called him by an unflattering nickname that was a bastardization of his last name. He looked me in the eye: "Don't call me that!" I never did again.

I think our friendship sprouted partially from my admiration and envy. I recall riding in my parents' car down Main St. in our hometown and seeing Dan playing drums in a rock band outside on the sidewalk. I was impressed, drawn to the beats.

As freshmen, we began hanging around together. He set his sights on an attractive girl in our high school, and soon, they were a couple. "*Any* guy can get *any* girl," he said, "you just have to know what to do." It certainly didn't hurt that Dan was the only percussionist who knew how to play the trap set. When he played with the jazz band, heads rotated toward him. Everyone had seen trumpet and sax players, but someone playing the drum set was a new phenomenon in our high school, which, at that time, did not even own a trap set. He seemed a walking embodiment of a dimension of the American Dream: that youthful confidence and optimism, that conviction that good fortune was winking at him, his big smile oozing bravado.

Our high school gym teacher, Mr. Page, who thought himself an army drill sergeant, would line us up and then bark: "Squad, attention! Dress, right, dress!" (I'm only now realizing "attention" was probably the actual word he used, but back then it sounded like, "Ten, hut!"). At the beginning of class, Mr. Page made us do calisthenics. We would count, "one, two, three, four" as we exercised, him strolling in front of us as we labored. When he wanted us to finally stop, he would say, "five, six, seven, eight," and we would cease on eight. One day, we had just begun doing jumping jacks when I heard Dan's voice pierce through: "five, six, seven, eight." Everyone stopped. Mr. Page wasn't happy with Dan, but he didn't get in trouble.

Gym class didn't always go badly. One year, playing badminton, Dan and I beat two of the best athletes in the school. Afterward, Dan ran around, racket in hand, yelling, "The freaks beat the jocks!"

In some ways, it was an unlikely friendship. He was an extrovert, and I was an introvert. He was conservative, and I was not. He told me I had been brainwashed by "The People's Republic of Madison." He thought Rush Limbaugh was just a funny guy rather than thinking he was, as I did, a dangerous voice. One that said out of one side of his mouth: Isn't the world a funny, strange place? From the other side, spewed all kinds of nastiness that people who were not thoughtful might take like a fish takes a worm.

While I admired Dan, I didn't idolize him. I saw another side, too. Sometimes I couldn't tell whether it grew out of good-natured mischievousness or something mean-spirited. Once, in high school, a friend of a friend who lived up north drove an hour to our town to buy some weed. Dan showed him a bag of stems and leaped into salesman mode, talking about how great they were. There were a few of us there, but no one said anything. I can't remember why now. Maybe

Dan asked us not to give away the scam. Maybe we were all just too stoned to care about speaking up. At any rate, the guy ended up paying good money for a bag of stems.

Afterward, Dan laughed, incredulous that the guy had fallen for the act. He took more delight, however, in the staging of the play itself than in the box office receipts. Another time, when my girlfriend had left some of her artwork, a clay plate, in his car, he told me how his brother's college friends had laughed at it. Another time, several of us were trying to find a place to camp on Memorial Day weekend. It was dark, and we were running out of possibilities. Dan sped us along winding forest roads.

"Hey man, slow down."

"Why?"

"Well, because there are deer, for one thing. If one leaped out in front of you, you wouldn't be able to stop."

"That won't be a problem."

"Why not?"

"Because I'm driving too fast for any deer to jump in front of my car."

There again was the self-confidence and bravado, only now, it seemed to border on lunacy. I doubt he believed what he was saying, but at the time, it seemed he did. We were lucky; we didn't have an accident, and we found a campsite.

Junior year was rough for Dan. He learned he had epilepsy. Before the diagnosis, he used to experience what he called "staring moods." He told me how cool they were and even wanted to try to teach me how to have one. He didn't understand they were actually petit mal seizures. Once, during English class he had one. When the teacher called on him, he just gazed into space, expressionless. The entire class looked at him. We called his name, but he was oblivious. Finally, he snapped out of it. A few weeks later, he suffered a grand mal seizure at home one morning before school and ended up in the hospital. I visited him there. He was perfectly normal, although it seemed odd to see him in his pajamas. Something changed for him at that point. He did not change. He had to take a couple pills every day. He didn't behave any differently, and I don't think he even felt different, but something changed.

His girlfriend left him for another guy, one who, coincidentally, had been one of my good friends during grade school, although we no longer hung out together. It was a bizarre situation. Apparently, the other guy had been "making time" with Dan's girl behind his back. He had well established himself with her. So, one day, he confronted Dan in the hallway. Dan liked to wear his hair longer than most, and this guy grabbed him by the hair, threw him on to the floor, and warned him not to bother her anymore. After that, we went over to my house. Dan was terribly upset, and I got him to write down his feelings, thinking that might help. That was the first time I think I had seen him low. He was crushed, not only by his girlfriend dumping him but by the assault in the hallway, which he saw as a public humiliation. He rebounded, though, and found another attractive girl to accompany him to prom. I admired him for that.

After high school, we spent less time together. He attended a state university about an hour away while I went to a local college. After that, I went to graduate school, then moved across the state. Whenever I went back home to see my family, one of the first things I would do was call Dan. We could spend hours together just sitting and talking, smoking cigarettes, drinking some coffee or a beer or two. My wife joked that we conversed without looking at each other. Instead, we talked while staring at the TV screen, our eyes on the Brewers, the Bucks, or some football game.

It had always felt to me that lucky things frequently happened to Dan, or that the universe accommodated him. In high school, one of his grandparents died, and he was the lucky recipient of a 1968 Belair with very few miles on it. Officially, the car belonged to the family, but he drove it all the time. Years later, he told me about walking through the mall near his workplace when he was still single. A young woman, who was doing some kind of survey, came up to him. They ended up in bed together that afternoon. There were other stories. An ex stopped over to say hello. Once inside his house, she started taking off her clothes. As a kid, he said he had played in a tree behind his house. There was a rock pile beneath the tree. One day, he slipped off the branch he was climbing on, but instead of ending up impaled on the jagged rocks beneath him, his pants caught on another limb, and there he hung in the air, upside down.

As an adult, he called up the famous ex-Packer Don Hutson and asked him if he would be willing to sign some autographs for him. Mr. Hutson said sure, so Dan mailed the photos to him, and in a few days, received, in the mail, autographed photos of one of the greatest NFL players ever.

In 2008, the economy tanked because of a surplus of wishful thinking, and it was trouble for Dan as well. He had worked as a headhunter but didn't like the management in the company he worked for, so he went out on his own. He did very well the first year, but the next year, following the crash, he had absolutely no income. I didn't realize his dire straits at the time, but I wondered whether he was having some trouble. He seldom showed interest in going out. When we did go out, he drank little. If we went to see a band, he would nurse a bottle of Bud Light for an entire set of music or more. I saw him only a few times a year. When I asked him how work was going, he would always tell me it was fine but never went into any details. He eventually had to borrow money from his family to live, but I think he was evasive even with them. Once, I was out at his folks' house with his younger brother. Dan wasn't there, but I recall his father shaking his head. "What does Danny do there at his house all day?" The luck seemed to have run out. He had what sounded like a great gig playing around town with his brother, who was a gifted pianist, and an excellent bass player, but Dan said the bass player would become anxious about playing live and would behave irrationally. So, the group broke up.

Near Thanksgiving Day, Dan walked down to the basement in the ranch home where he lived alone and shot himself with a handgun. A day or two before, we had spoken on the phone. *Monday Night Football* was on, and I had called him just to chat for a bit before my wife got home from work. As I spoke about the game I was watching, he turned on his television and watched, too, so that even though we were hundreds of miles apart, we were in that familiar position of watching television together and talking without looking at each other. When my wife came home, we hung up.

In a high school class, he once had discussed the question, "Is our experience in life basically a solitary one, or are we defined by our relationships with others?" (Had I been in the class, I would have answered "solitary" as Dan's classmate who would later become my girlfriend did.) Dan, however, insisted the opposite was true. His death shocked me for that reason but also because I had thought of him as someone who was always in control, who was direct about things, who minced no words, and who, if others were paralyzed or uncertain, would act boldly. And yet, now I see that all those qualities may have contributed to his final act.

There were hints, the retrospective foreshadowing I suppose most people torment themselves with after someone they love commits suicide. There was the not-wanting-to-go-out or not wanting to drink much beer, although there was never any stinginess on his part, despite his lack of money.

One time, when we were alone up north at his family's cabin, he talked about how he wished he could just hide up there. While I generally shared that sentiment, I remember thinking that was an odd way to put it. The summer before he died, he drove 255 miles to visit me. We hung around together at my house. I recall sitting on the swings in our back yard and chatting aimlessly. Somehow, we got to talking about women, and he mentioned that he figured he had been with over thirty of them in his life. There were many fish in his sea, but I attempted to divert his attention, suggesting that we would be able to do some fishing in the river near my house, which is what we always did when he visited. After being at my house for only a few hours, however, he told me he had to get back home. I don't recall him giving any reason. I tried to talk him out of it, but he set on the idea that he couldn't stay. So, he got in his car and drove back home. During our final conversation, when I told him I had to get going, he said, "okay." It was the most forlorn tone I had ever heard in his voice. It was a tone of complete surrender. The next day, I thought about it and decided I should call him and find out whether he was okay. All I got was a voice message. I tried calling him repeatedly in the following days, but I never got through. I don't know when he shot himself, but I hope it wasn't after we hung up the phone that night.

I am thankful I can distract myself from thoughts about the hows and whys by remembering the many kind things he did for me over the years.

He helped me fix up an old drum set I've had since high school. He found the parts on eBay and mailed them to me. He took me bass fishing on a few lakes and fly-fishing for smallmouth bass on the Fox River. He told me that if I was willing to drive across the state and accompany him to his cabin, he guaranteed I would catch the biggest trout in my life (it was 18 inches long, and I released it). He took me to a Packers game on Christmas. Back in high school, he had tried to show me how to drive stick (I tried without success until he was afraid I would grind his Belair's transmission into pieces). He tried to show me how to trap shoot (I was 0 for 10). He brought my daughter gifts when we visited. In his suicide note, he said he wanted me to have his 1960s Ludwig Supraphonic snare drum (the one I had seen him playing that day I rode down Main Street) because he knew I would play it instead of selling it. I still play that drum.

I recall one of the first times I used it after he died. I was playing music that always wore me out after a few sets, Led Zeppelin, Deep Purple, Hendrix. There was an up-tempo Zeppelin song that kicked my ass every time we practiced it, but that night, as I was playing it, I felt an extraordinary energy. I remember thinking to myself that it was as if Dan were there bringing his, keeping me going. The law of conservation of energy states that energy is never lost; it only changes form.

In the end, I believe Dan felt he had hit too many dead ends. There were two failed marriages. His once-successful career would no longer support him. He was in debt. And when things went badly, Dan was hard on himself.

I was over at his house with his younger brother a few days after he died. I went down to his basement, where Dan shot himself. He would always take me down there to show me a newly acquired percussion equipment or to play his drums. There was a drain in the middle of the floor. All signs of violent death had been scrubbed away, except for a blood stain near that drain. I stared at it, unable to help myself. As we went through Dan's closet, looking at his clothes, I noticed the bed wasn't made. From the bedside table, I picked up a small radio with earphones. The radio was still on. And then, my morbid imagination began to wind out a tale: he'd woken up with the immediate thought that he was right back where he was before sleep had floated him off to some faraway, kinder place. "F*#k it," I imagined him saying as he left the radio on and set it down on the table before crawling out of bed and leaving it unmade, grabbing his gun, and heading downstairs to the basement.

Strange fact: Dan was the third guy in my high school class to kill himself. Stranger, one of the others was the guy who stole his girlfriend. In the years since Dan died, I have sometimes wondered whether I depended too much on his friendship: to the point that I didn't care about making or renewing others. It's as though I took all my cash and put it in a stock that failed. But I suppose I will always feel that I failed, too. I'm lucky to be able to say that I can count on one hand the number of suicides I have known, but I also feel fortunate that, on the other hand, I am able to count friends I have loved.

PART II

UNSPOKEN

Houses are not haunted. We are haunted, and regardless of the architecture with which we surround ourselves, our ghosts stay with us until we ourselves are ghosts.

—Dean Koontz

5

GAIL AND THE SPECIAL SEARS SALE

TERRI ELDERS

Gail exuded a kind of early 1950s sophistication that most of my Los Angeles ninth-grade cronies could admire, but never hope to emulate. First, she always wore mascara and eyeliner. Second, she not only smoked Kools, she also carried them in a gold-plated case with a matching Ronson lighter. Third, she dressed in straight skirts so tight that she hobbled.

So that Friday, when Gail asked me if I'd like to go shopping with her after school, I responded with delighted surprise. Though we lived on the same block, Gail had never been one of the neighborhood gang who at sunset played kick-the-can or our reverse of hide-and-seek, sardines. Occasionally, she'd lounge on her porch and watch the rest of us scrambling across hedges to retrieve an errant can or scurrying in search of a staked-out group hiding place.

I'd been stuffing my zippered loose-leaf binder into my locker when Gail approached. "Hey, Ter, I'm going shopping this afternoon. Sears and Roebuck is having a special sale. Wanna come with me?" Since I didn't have any reason to excuse myself, I agreed to go. Might be fun and I might be able to pick up some tips about selecting lipstick.

"Well, yes," I agreed, "but I don't have much money."

"Don't worry. I have some, and I'll treat you to a cherry Coke at Owl Drugstore after."

We wandered down Vermont towards Slauson, pausing to gaze into the windows of Lerner's and Mode O'Day. Even though my dad worked as a shoe salesman at Sears on Friday night and Saturdays, his moonlighting job, I rarely visited the store, but Gail had said there was a collection of cashmere sweaters and some new costume jewelry she wanted to see. For me, shopping without my mom as chaperone was a novelty.

As we neared the Woolworth's, Gail grabbed my elbow. "You're interested in lipstick, aren't you? Let's go in here for a minute."

Indeed, I had a secret tube of Pink Queen, worn almost to a nub. Now that I was in the last year of junior high, I felt compelled to apply a touch every morning as soon as I left the house. My parents had forbidden makeup until high school, but most of my classmates were already sporting some. I had skipped third grade, so at thirteen, I was a year behind in age, which gave me a stronger incentive for wanting to appear a little more mature.

We paused at the makeup counter, and I stood entranced as Gail showed me how to use the samples—applying just a smidgeon on my wrist to see how each hue would look on me. The salesclerk approached, and Gail smiled at her.

"We're just looking," she said, taking my elbow and steering me towards the door.

At the Sears store, we stopped at the lingerie counter to look at the latest styles in sheer denier nylons. Clocking was the latest fad, with embroidered hearts and other designs at the ankle. Though I still wore oxfords and bobby socks, I was hoping to get a garter belt and stockings to go with my promised graduation suit and Cuban heeled pumps, as well.

At the jewelry counter, Gail and I each tried on several pairs of earrings, clips for her and hoops for me. I'd been proud that my grandmother had pierced my ears when I was only eight.

"Nothing particularly terrific here," Gail said with disdain, sweeping aside the jewelry we had examined. "Time to head for the sportswear."

Two men loomed over us, grabbing each of us by a wrist. "You're not heading anywhere except to the basement with us."

Gasping, I stared at Gail. She smiled wanly at the man who had seized her.

I couldn't mimic her aplomb. "Who are you? What's happening?" I stuttered, struggling to free my hand from the tight grip of the man next to me.

"You know who we are. Did you think this was a five-finger discount store?" Though I then realized the pair must be floorwalkers prowling for shoplifters, I remained bewildered until we got to the basement office, when the men opened our purses and shook out the contents.

My tiny clutch held my handkerchief, pencils, bobby pins, a comb, and a few pennies. Gail's larger shoulder bag yielded a treasure trove of items, most of them startlingly familiar: two lipsticks, still in their packaging, three sets of earrings, and a pair of stockings.

Horrified, I looked up at each of the men and then at Gail and started to bawl. "I didn't know," I protested. "My dad works here at Sears. I would never steal anything. I didn't know."

"That's hard to believe," the men chorused. "What's your dad's name? Let's get him down here right now."

"Oh, no," I wailed. My father had a notorious temper, and I cringed, thinking of the shouting that was about to ensue, and the thrashing I would suffer when I got home.

Gail knew my dad and had heard him hollering at kids who had crashed into our hedge with their bikes. "Wait a minute," she said. The floorwalkers looked at her.

"She didn't know I was swiping stuff," Gail explained. "She's telling the truth. Let her go."

The men looked at each other and then at me. I emitted another sniff and sob, reaching towards the meager pile of my possessions for my hankie.

"Go home," they chorused. I walked home alone, shaking all the way.

Gail never returned to school. I heard through the neighborhood grapevine that she had transferred to another junior high a few miles away. Though I spotted her on her porch now and then, when I waved, she'd turn around and walk back into her house.

I had wanted to reassure her that I really didn't know she'd been pilfering. But I never got the chance. To this day, I'm convinced she thought she was protecting me because of my dad's reputation for a quick temper, not because she believed I was naïve to the point of oblivion.

The next year, when I started high school, I got a job as a waitress at the Owl Drugstore counter, across from Sears. On my breaks, I'd always make myself a cherry Coke and plan what I would buy with my weekly paycheck: lipstick, earrings, and sometimes even an on-sale cashmere sweater. I never tried for a five-finger discount.

I always hoped Gail would come into the drugstore, but she never did. I would have offered to buy her a cherry Coke. She introduced me to dangerous adventure and to courageous honesty. She paid a price that I would never suffer because of my intimate proximity to her adolescent crime. In one afternoon, she taught me just about everything I needed to know about dishonor and honor. I hope she would not be embarrassed to see me now. I still want to thank her.

6

WHAT I DIDN'T SAY

PAT HALE

I was going to say that six years ago, I was to go to the theater with my friend Laura to see a play about a man and woman buried up to their necks in sand. I was going to say that I had forgotten the name — it was a famous play of the absurd; a childish, strident Estelle Parsons played the female lead. I think she wore a hat with big flowers, and read from a tube of toothpaste, and maybe they got out of the sand at the end, and perhaps they didn't. I was going to say that I didn't recall what seemed to be a key point in the narrative flow, but that I did remember my sister standing in for Laura at the last moment when she called to say she wasn't well.

I was going to say all this. But last week, when I was once again at the Hartford Stage, walking along the upper lobby at intermission, sipping my drink and looking at the pictures of previous shows, I found myself in front of a photo from the play I was to see with Laura. I can no longer plead ignorance, for the photograph was labeled; the play was "Happy Days" by Samuel Beckett. I pulled a napkin from my bag and wrote the name of the play, and then stood staring at it, at Estelle Parsons' bland face, trying to fill in from that photograph all the missing details of the play. The photo began to trigger recollection. Apparently, not many people take notes from the photos, for I caught the floor manager's attention. She spoke to me for a few minutes, and then offered me the poster from the show. It was not on display, but she had it in back. I flattened it out at home and was initially disappointed, as it didn't show the pile of sand clearly, just a mirror sticking out of the sand. Then I thought, how metaphorical to see a mirror buried in the sand, to see one's reflection through the entrapment. And I wanted to know more.

When I think back, I don't remember many details from the production. I remember thinking, as I watched it, that Laura would have loved it. I remember that my sister did not. I remember the details well because that weekend we learned that Laura had cancer. Even now, months after her death, writing those words makes my hands freeze on the keyboard, makes me stare into an invisible horizon. But at the time we watched the play, I felt regret that she wasn't with me, but I wasn't worried because she was often sick or suddenly responsible for watching grandchildren, and plans were often broken. It wasn't until the next day that the phone call came. And then things were never the same again —period. But back to the play. Always back to the play, or the kids, or world events—anything to keep from acknowledging the finality of the loss that occurs when a dear friend, this dear friend, dies. I borrowed a copy of the play from the library and carried it around for a while, thinking it would give me a framework from which I could understand Laura's death, or at least a framework from which to discuss it (Why was the woman in the sand? Why did the sand get deeper? Does the sand always get deeper? Are we inevitably buried by our lives?). But I never opened it because I knew that the understanding had to come from within me.

I keep the poster in my workroom now, tacked to a bulletin board, over the previous levels of newspaper cartoons and photographs that have been there so long that I no longer see them. I do see the poster every time I look up from my work. In the way the recently bereaved judge themselves, I am always ready to feel guilty. Sometimes, when I find myself studying Estelle's image in the mirror, I'm concerned that my focus has shifted from the subject at hand —saying goodbye and holding on to Laura—to a selfish interest in a play. I am afraid that I am looking for anything to focus on to avoid thinking about that which is difficult to see. How often did I focus on the unimportant aspects of daily life, and how often did I refuse to hear or see what was before me in hideously personal detail? How often did I allow my focus to shift so that Laura's pain couldn't transfer to me?

Estelle's face looks different to me from day to day. Sometimes her expression is bovine and blank; sometimes she seems fearful. How could she not be afraid, finding herself trapped and unable to escape the world collapsed around her body—the world that had shrunk to a single hill? How could Laura not have been afraid? And how could I, in turn, have not set my own fear aside to ask her about her own?

Laura never spoke to me of her fear. At times, she addressed her illness with grim humor, perhaps taking some pleasure from the shock value of making an offhand reference to the fact that at least she wouldn't be around long enough to see some future entanglement unfold. This I swallowed as best I could, accepting it as honorable medicine, the price paid for being thought strong enough to shoulder that small portion of someone else's troubles. Towards the end, occasionally, she vented her frustration at the unfairness that I had an exciting life unfolding ahead of me, was talking of graduate school, of traveling to Korea to teach English, while she did not. I could do anything I wanted, while she would die and never know what happened next, never see family milestones. I ignored these comments until no more were offered. My failure to listen is a source of guilt and grief to me, this and the realization that, at her funeral, I resented the others with claims to her. How childish I found myself to be! I embraced the family and tolerated the friends who had come before me, the girlhood chums who had shared her adolescence, but I could not bear those who came after me or concurrent with me. I wanted her to myself.

The only forgiveness I find for myself is the suspicion that she recognized my jealousy, that she understood it, accepted it, and perhaps even found it touching and amusing. When I think of the memorial service, I imagine the church filled with jealous souls, sitting alone, shoulder to shoulder, sharing Kleenex and the flickering knowledge that, in the end, we were strong enough to say goodbye but not big enough to share. We listened to each other's tributes, judging the degree of intimacy revealed by the anecdotes shared at the pulpit. We glanced sideways to see who was crying and who was getting up the nerve to speak. She would have loved it. She was always ready to let me see how silly I was being. She would have been at my elbow, at all our elbows, swirling around us trying to get us to sing one more round of her favorite childhood song, to get up and dance one last hokey-pokey. She would have requested balloons. She would have demanded our attention, reminded us that she was the one who was dead and that this was her day, not ours.

This is her greatest legacy to me: the lesson that while she had lost her life, I had not lost a friend. She is still with me, mocking me when I am my most ridiculous and telling me to face the truth and move on. She would say it is okay to wallow for a moment if it makes you feel involved, but then get up out of the mud, brush yourself off, and move on to something that matters, like checking out the neighbors' flowers or eating an egg sandwich or reading.

One Christmas, Laura gave all her female friends a book by Sharon Olds because it contained a short poem called "The Pope's Penis." She was so delighted with the poem that she made me open the gift immediately, and then stood and watched me read it, practically exploding with excitement. One of her friends put a copy of the poem in the casket with her, alongside the letters from her grandchildren, her husband's first ponytail, and lots of wildflowers. I was immensely cheered up to see the poem there and wondered which woman had put it there. I wish it had been me. And acknowledging that last word of jealousy, I smile, forgive myself, and go out to do something important, something exciting, something that matters.

7

SAM AND LELOR

ADRIENNE PINE

As a child, I liked opening the pages of our local phone book and studying the long lists of names. My mother confessed that when she was a child, she and her brother used the telephone directory to call local pharmacies. "Do you have Prince Albert in the can?" she'd ask the clerk who answered the phone, referring to a popular chewing tobacco. If the clerk said yes, then she'd say, "Well, let him out; he can't breathe," dissolving into giggles as she hung up. Less benign was her and her brother's practice of calling up coal companies and asking for a truckload delivery to a random address. Sometimes the address was an actual residence, and sometimes it wasn't.

"You mean they'd actually deliver coal to someone who hadn't ordered it?" I'd ask, and my mother would nod, her eyes still laughing at the memory.

"Did they ever find out it was you?"

She shook her head. "Not usually." Only once was she

found out, and that was the end of it. I think my mother wanted to shock me. She knew that I would never have thought of doing something like that.

"How would you and your brother know what happened to the deliveries?" I asked my mother.

"We wouldn't."

———

It was a long, leisurely, imaginative play. We spent a long time setting up our fantasy world, arranging the house and furniture, organizing doll clothes. Katie was Barbie, and I was Midge, and we'd be forever changing their outfits, getting them ready for the activities of their busy lives. Skipper was a part of the entourage, and Ken was Barbie's boyfriend

What was the fun in that? I wondered.

Yet, my mother's confession inspired me to delve deeper into the telephone directory. I found a willing accomplice in my friend Katie. Katie lived up the street, and during our childhood, we spent many weekends together. I would usually go to her house because she had a room of her own. We loved to play Barbie, and she had all the Barbie accoutrements —not only Barbie and Ken but outfits galore for them, as well as Barbie's Dream House and furniture. I'd bring over Skipper and Midge, Barbie's little sister and her friend, and we'd play all weekend.

Playing Barbie was an all-weekend affair, and we took breaks. During the day, Katie and I practiced shooting baskets into the hoop attached to the garage. Sometimes it was just the two of us, and sometimes Katie's brother Pete and his friend Otis joined us. On Saturday nights, Katie's parents usually went out, and Katie and I would sneak Cokes from the kitchen, which we kept on ice in her bathroom sink, as we holed ourselves up in her room for a long Barbie session. In the morning, we'd resume where we left off the night before.

One day, during one of our breaks, I told her about my pastime of reading the telephone directory, and we decided to read it together. Katie found her family's copy and brought it back to her room. We sat cross-legged on the floor with it open in front of us. First, we found our families' listings and the families of our friends. As we turned the pages, we gazed at the long lists of common names, like "Jones" and "Smith," and found uncommon ones, like "Hershkovitz."

We talked about what you could tell about a person from his or her name. Since we were both Jewish, we recognized the Jewish names. Some of the people attached to Jewish names we knew personally. But what about other names? Was it possible, we wondered, to tell whether people were white or black from their names? Sometimes it was, we decided, and sometimes it wasn't.

It was the early 1960s, the time of civil rights demonstrations, and we were living in the epicenter of it all, Birmingham, Alabama. Our suburb "over the mountain" was segregated, and we had almost no connection with black people other than the maids and yardmen who worked for our families. We barely spoke to the yardmen, who came infrequently and worked outdoors, but our connections to our families' maids were close and intimate. We loved Marion and May, who worked for Katie's family, and Georgia and Selma Lee, who worked for mine. We followed them around the house, watching them while they worked, until they shooed us away. Mostly we loved listening to the way they talked and what they said. When Katie and I were alone together, we tried to imitate them.

We recognized that while they knew all about our lives, we knew extraordinarily little about theirs. Even as a child, I sensed that it was hard for them to be open and honest about their feelings with white people. Katie and I saw it all the time in the interactions between them and our mothers. It was true even with us children. Like the polluted haze that hung over the city of Birmingham, hatred and violence were in the atmosphere we breathed. How did they live with it, and how did they survive it? I wondered. None of them owned cars, and to get to our houses, they had to take long meandering bus rides across the city and over the mountain.

When the maids in our neighborhood walked to and from the bus stop to our houses, they armed themselves with sticks against the dogs that ran free because there was no leash law. They weren't the vicious German Shepherd attack dogs that Birmingham's public safety commissioner, Bull Connor, let loose on the civil rights demonstrators. They were ordinary neighborhood pets like our Cocker Spaniel, Taffy, and Katie's Schnauzer, Peppy, but they were spirited, territorial, and ran in a pack. The maids complained, but there was nothing they could do other than wield sticks to shoo the dogs away.

The neighborhood dogs were only one of the many indignities they had to live with daily. I wondered about the aspects of their lives that remained separate from us. What did they do when they weren't with us?

Sometimes we had glimpses. Someone had given Katie half a dozen chicks in the spring, and Katie fell in love with them. Katie's mother allowed her to keep them in a box in the laundry room, and Katie fed them and gave them water and cleaned the box.

The chicks grew quickly. One day they were precious little balls of downy yellow feathers that walked around unsteadily, and one day they were too big for the box, and Katie's mother told her they couldn't keep them anymore. May agreed to take them. Her son came in his car to pick her up, along with the chicks. Katie was in tears when they drove away.

Time went by, and one day Katie asked May about the chicks. May told Katie they were very good. "What do you mean?" asked Katie, confused by the use of the past tense. "You don't still have them?"

"No, ma'am," replied May.

"Why not?" asked Katie.

"Well, I ate 'em," said May.

"What! All of them?"

"Yes, I did, and they were dee-licious."

To Katie, the chicks were pets, but to May, they were food. In horror and fascination, Katie listened to May described how she had chased each chick around the back-yard, caught it, and wrung its neck. Over time, she killed each one, plucked it, dressed it, cooked it, and ate it, until they were all gone.

Katie was in shock. She realized that May assumed that she knew that the chickens would be eaten. It would not have occurred to May to do anything else with them.

Small and wiry, with gray hair and coffee-colored skin, May was older than Marion, Georgia, or Selma Lee. Katie's family's house had a maid's room with its own small bathroom that opened off one side of the laundry room. May came on the weekends when Marion was off, and she stayed over on Saturday night, while Katie's parents went out. May had asked Katie's parents to buy her own television set, and after she gave us supper and cleaned the kitchen, she retreated to her room, where she watched TV with the curtains drawn and the door closed. Her room was her sanctum, and it was forbidden to disturb her there except for an emergency. We never had an emergency. Katie and I stayed in her room playing Barbie, and Katie's two brothers played in their room.

One Saturday afternoon Katie and I were reading the telephone directory, looking for interesting names. I had excellent eyesight and was good at scanning the long lists in small print, whereas Katie had a learning disability that would be diagnosed as dyslexia and require her to do daily eye exercises. I took over, scanning the names and reading the interesting ones aloud to Katie. I went first to letters of the alphabet with the fewer names, like "I" and "U." Then I went to "H," "J," and "K." When I got tired of those letters, I went to "S." "S" was such a substantial, satisfying letter. The lists of names beginning with "S" went on for pages and pages. I flipped through them, and then I saw something that caught my eye, that I had never seen before.

"That's odd."

"What?" asked Katie.

"Here are two people listed, a man and a woman, with the same last name, the same address, and the same telephone number. Do you think they are married? Usually, when people are married, there is only one listing with the husband's name. That's the way it is in your family and my family. So, if they are married, why are they both listed, and why are the listings on separate lines?"

"I don't know," replied Katie. "Can I see it?"

"Here," I pointed with my index finger. "Here's 'Sneed, Lelor,' and right underneath her is 'Sneed, Sam.' See, they have the same address, '1501 Trilby,' and the same phone number, 'TR8-9591.'"

"Yeah, you're right," Katie agreed. "I wonder." She paused. "Maybe they're brother and sister, and they live together."

"Maybe," I considered. "If they were brother and sister, it makes sense they'd want their own listings."

"Where is Trilby?"

"I have no idea."

"Not in our suburb?"

"I never heard of it."

"Me neither. Do you think they're Negroes?"

"I do. Sam could be anybody, but Lelor sounds like a Negro name."

"Let's call them," said Katie suddenly.

"But what'll we say? Who will we tell them we are? They won't want to talk to two white kids."

"We'll tell them we're their neighbors. We'll tell them we live down the street."

"What'll we talk about?"

"I don't know. Anything. We can talk about the trouble we have with our 'chirren,'" said Katie, pronouncing the word the way we'd heard Marion pronounce it."

We ended up chickening out of calling Sam and Lelor. Yet, I thought about them, and so did Katie. One afternoon, several weeks later, when we were together at Katie's house, we got out the phone book again and looked them up. The double listing was not an apparition. On an impulse, before I could change my mind, I dialed the number. The sound of the jangling telephone quickened my nerves. I thought of hanging up, but before I could, a deep, resonant male voice answered.

"Hello."

I was holding the receiver away from my ear, so Katie could listen in, too, and I almost dropped it. To us, the voice sounded like it belonged to a black man.

"Hello," he repeated patiently.

"Hey, hey," I began haltingly, trying to make my voice sound as much like May, Georgia, or Selma Lee as I could. "Hey, is this Sam?" I asked.

"Ye-es."

"And are you married to Lelor?" I hazarded.

"Yes, I am. Who is this?"

"Well, I'm Ma-ry," pronouncing it like I'd heard Georgia pronounce her sister's name, with a long "a" and emphasis on both syllables. "I'm your neighbor lady. I live down the street. I see you two pass by, and I thought I'd call and introduce myself to you. Is Lelor there?"

"No, she went out."

"Well, I'd like to introduce myself to her. I'll call back another time. Thank you for speaking with me. Good afternoon," I said.

"Good afternoon," he replied, and I hung up, replacing the receiver in its cradle.

"Did you hear that?" I exclaimed to Katie. "He talked to us. He really talked to us."

"Do you think he thought you were Mary, the lady down the street?"

"I don't know. What do you think?"

"I don't know."

"I don't think I sounded very convincing," I said.

"I don't think so either," Katie agreed.

"I still want to call again and talk to Lelor."

Katie wasn't certain she did, but I persuaded her. The next week we called back, and this time Lelor answered.

"This is Ma-ry, your neighbor lady down the street. I'm with my friend Florence. Did Sam tell you we called?"

"He may have mentioned it." Lelor's voice was soft, hesitant.

Searching for a topic of conversation, I brought up the weather. In my experience, grown-ups loved talking about the weather.

"With all this rain we've been having, I got pains in my joints," I confessed to Lelor, remembering one of Selma Lee's complaints. "I declare, I can hardly lift my right arm."

"That's a pity," replied Lelor. "I do hope you be feeling better soon."

"At least it's not raining now."

"That would be the waste of a good day."

"It sure would. Thank you for talking to me. I tell you what, next time I see you coming down the street, I'll wave."

"You have a nice day, then."

"You, too."

After we hung up, I was elated.

"I can't believe she really talked to us," I said to Katie.

"They both did," said Katie.

"I want to call them again."

"I do, too."

Over the next few months, we talked to Sam and Lelor more than half a dozen times. We discussed the weather, the neighborhood, hard times and good times, sickness and health, and we tried out phrases and exclamations we had heard spoken by Marion, May, Georgia, or Selma Lee. My favorite was "Lord have mercy on my soul!" That was what Marion said when she was worked up.

Sam and Lelor were polite and reticent. They didn't challenge or question us or get carried away. To this day, I don't know what they thought of us. They never refused to talk to us, although sometimes they begged off because of household chores that needed to be done. In return, we invented household chores for ourselves. I took my cues from them. One of my favorite conversations with Lelor was when she told me how she cleaned her oven with baking soda and vinegar. Once, Katie asked why both of their names were in the phone book. "I'm a person, too," replied Lelor. "I want to see my own name there."

What she said made sense to us, although we'd never thought about it before.

As we grew fonder of them, our affection struggled with our guilt. We were living a lie. We were quite sure that had we told them who we really were, they never would have talked to us.

One Saturday evening, after Katie's parents had gone out, we unplugged Katie's mother's princess phone and took it in Katie's bedroom where there was a jack waiting for the day when Katie would have her own phone. While we talked to Sam and Lelor in Katie's room, May was in her room watching television. What would May have said had she known what we were doing? Without a doubt, we knew that she would disapprove and scold us for "fooling around." To us, it didn't feel like fooling around. We were trying to make a connection, but it was founded on a falsehood. There was nowhere for us to go with Sam and Lelor, and eventually our conversations petered out. We stopped calling them and turned to other enthusiasms. Sam and Lelor slipped from our thoughts.

Two years passed. Katie and I were now twelve years old, in junior high. We had put Barbie and all her accoutrements away, and we no longer spent our weekends setting up our imaginary Barbie world and playing out our Barbie fantasies.

In our school, the students were divided between the popular people—the boys who played sports and the girls who were cheerleaders—and everyone else. We faced social pressures we were powerless to resist. Everyone, it seemed, had to be part of a clique. Between classes, the Jewish kids often walked down the hallways together, and sometimes, if no teachers were around, some tough boys would come after us, scattering pennies at our feet as they commanded us, "Pick 'em up, Jews" in hostile tones. We kept on walking as if we hadn't noticed them. I worried our tormentors would pursue us, but so far, they hadn't.

I hadn't thought about Sam and Lelor for ages, when one day they popped into my mind. I was over at Katie's house when I had an urge to call them. Katie wasn't sure she wanted to.

"What'll we say?" she wondered. "How will we explain why we stopped calling them?"

"We'll tell them we moved. We'll tell them that we were thinking about them."

"I don't know."

"Oh, come on, Katie."

"All right. But you call."

"I still know their telephone number — TR8-9591."

"Okay."

Though I had been eager to call, I hesitated after I dialed the number, but I didn't hang up. After several rings, Sam answered the phone. I recognized his voice, though it seemed to me that he didn't quite sound like himself.

"Sam, Sam, this is Ma-ry. Remember me? I used to live down the street, but I moved away. That's why you haven't heard from me. But I'm here with my friend Florence, and we been thinking about you. We decided to call you."

I waited for Sam to reply, but he didn't. I tried again.

"This is Ma-ry, and my friend Florence is with me. We used to talk from time to time. Then I moved away. But we wanted to let you know we missed talking to you. How you doing, Sam? How's Lelor?"

Sam didn't respond. I repeated my question. "Well," he said finally, after a pause, "Lelor is dead."

"What?" I forgot to try to sound like our maids. I was in shock. "No, no. I didn't know. I'm so sorry. I had no idea."

"The cancer done took her," he said. "It's been more than a year now. It's mighty quiet here without her."

"Oh, no. We're so sorry. We're so sorry."

It was all Katie and I could do to apologize. We ended the conversation and hung up. A sense of shame overwhelmed us. We had pretended we were playing a game, but it wasn't a game. We were both so upset that we could barely speak of it to each other. We had trespassed on a private grief.

Afterwards, we got out the phone book, and I turned to "S," scanning the long lists of names. There it was, in black and white: "Sneed, Sam," but no Lelor. We remembered what Lelor had said about having her name in the phone book and being a person too.

We never called Sam again.

Over fifty years have passed since then—two generations. On paper at least, African Americans won their civil rights years ago, although, in practice, injustice, racism, and prejudice still intrude on their everyday lives. When Katie and I found Sam and Lelor in the phone book and called them, we did not intend to hurt them. We believed we were trying to make a connection. We told ourselves we were innocent, until we had to face the fact that we weren't.

Until now, I have never told anyone about Sam and Lelor. After all these years, Katie and I are still friends, yet we never talk about them. For me, they are a secret source of shame, harm I inflicted without meaning to. Playing Barbie was one thing, but playing imaginary games with people was quite another. We never resolved this deed. We never apologized. Never sent flowers. Never made amends. We never figured out what to do.

Previously published, Barely *South*, Spring 2019.

PART III

DIVERGENCE

Growing apart doesn't change the fact that for a long time we grew side by side; our roots will always be tangled. I'm glad for that.

—Ally Condie

8

SIX SNAPSHOTS

NANCY LONDON

What is it that I want you to know about her? When I met Emma, she was seventeen, and I was twenty-five, but in many ways, she was older, had already lived a bigger life. She grew up on the beach in Malibu; her daddy was a famous director, and her godfather, a two-time Oscar winner. She told me she could look out her bedroom window and see Marilyn wrapped in a shawl, taking her morning walk.

Daddy drove her to a progressive private school most mornings. Some mornings they swerved, headed north instead of east, played hooky together and didn't tell her mom.

She left home at fifteen with her parent's permission and moved up the coast to a beach bungalow in Santa Cruz her daddy owned. At fifteen, she married, also with her parent's permission, her eighteen-year-old boyfriend in a redwood grove, barefoot, with a crown of daisies in her hair.

I'll admit it; I was dazzled—Jay Gatsby kind of dazzled. She had a glow about her, a self-assurance I found unnerving. I had grown up in Queens, one of the boroughs of New York City, in a cluster of houses banged together after the war. Each home had one tree and two choices of floor plan. Would you like your living room here or here?

My daddy died of a heart attack when I was twelve and mom was forty-two. He left us with bills and no life insurance. We never went hungry, but the small ship carrying us across those grief-filled years constantly threatened to up end with the slightest wind. I wanted so much, a bigger house, a mother who noticed how badly I hurt, better clothes, and a father.

A mutual friend introduced us, and a day later Emma phoned to invite me to dinner. At first, I refused; what the hell would we even find to talk about? I felt shy and awkward but then called right back and said yes. She made dinner from her garden, baked her own bread, and flashed her long legs and blue eyes. Jesus. I had just arrived from the east coast, where I had been over-educated, over-f#*cked, and over-tired of my brain and the women's movement and all the PC things I should and shouldn't be doing.

We went out for drinks, sharing joints, sitting on her front steps watching the fog roll in, drinking scotch and smoking Shermans.

I made her laugh. In return, she said, "Tell me anything, and I will listen." We opened the jewel boxes of our sexual histories and drew out each gem, one at a time, and told each other the stories of one-night stands, the experiments with women, and the threesomes. No one living or dead knew how many there had been for each of us, and when we finished speaking, we would pack away the precious stones that held the wildness we felt safe sharing with each other. I told her about my illegal abortion, and she wept with me; I described the miscarriage when I hadn't known I was pregnant, the tiny fetus floating in the toilet before I flushed it away in horror.

Snapshot:

This is a picture of my pick-up truck. Emma and her husband were moving up to Oregon for a year. She said she'd leave a pile of compost for me in her yard, and several days after their departure, I corralled my dope dealer, Scotty, to come into town with me. The yard was bare. Nothing anywhere. See me standing there feeling small and stupid and ashamed for wanting.

By the time she came back to town a year later, I had married Scotty. It was good for a while, like things were back then in Santa Cruz. Still a small town, friendly people, lots of pot, and lots of good day sunshine. She divorced her husband and would only say, "It was time. It wasn't working out," and she began seeing her married professor with four kids and a wife who didn't see it coming. She pried him out of that marriage like you'd pry an abalone off a cliff at low tide, persistently, with a flat bar. She adopted his kids, and then they had one of their own.

Snapshot:

This is the hospital where they scraped me out. I miscarried twins at three months, stood ankle-deep in blood, holding on to chairs trying to get to the phone. I lay in the back of the cab, blood soaking through three towels at a time. They came for me with a stretcher and skated me down the corridor to a cold, bright room where I held on to the nurse's freckled arm while they removed the unsustainable. Scotty came to see me in my small semi-private room. He banged on the hospital bed in frustration; he needed to drive south that night to his massive greenhouse and water his marijuana cash crop. "Hey," I said, "I get your priorities. Go and don't ever come back." I served him with divorce papers two months later.

I called Emma. I needed to get home, and it was getting late. I could hear the party in the background. Em and her professor had moved up the hill to an impressive home her father owned. I vomited, trying to tell her where I was and what had happened. She understood me despite my stuttered and messy speech. I waited for her outside, crouched against the cold brick hospital wall. She hopped out of her car wearing a gorgeous silk dress and four-inch heels, smelling of Joy perfume. She hauled me into the car and drove me home, guided me carefully inside, the huge pad between my legs already soaked with blood, more blood. Blood for days to come. She tucked me in and shushed me when I tried to thank her. "It was a boring party," she said, but of course, it wasn't. She brought me iron-building foods the next day, and every day until I could stand on my own, until I could share a scotch and finally exhale.

Then we had fun. We led with our boobs and turned heads wherever we went, like Betty and Veronica on steroids, a long-legged blonde and voluptuous brunette. We shared our clothes, our pot, and money if one of us was temporarily broke, although her broke was different from mine. We wore the same size bra, and she had so many that it was easy to pass some along to me. Her mother would send her two bathrobes from some exclusive Beverly Hills store with a label that sounded like a private island or a secret club only the rich knew about. And I'd be glad to get the one Em didn't want since the one hanging on the back of my bathroom door looked like a prop for an Arthur Miller play. We'd take road trips up to Calistoga and slather ourselves in mud and drive down the coast for silent retreats at the Benedictine Monastery in Big Sur where we stayed up late in the courtyard whispering and laughing until one of the monks came to issue us a warning.

Then things got more complicated. She divorced the professor who managed to get her father's house in the settlement, and I married the gentle man I had known and loved for years. We moved out of town as Em was beginning an affair with a married man with two kids and a cool artist wife.

"Hey," I said tentatively on the phone, "What's with all the married men?" I could hear her bristle. "It's not like that," she said, but I thought it was. I remembered all the stories she had told me about the alliance she and her father had forged against her mother and the satisfaction Em had taken in being his chosen one, in beating the competition.

"Maybe talk to a therapist about it," I tentatively suggested. "Maybe I'll talk to you instead," she said, and I was dismayed, flattered, knowing I lacked the therapeutic skills needed to dig down into that swamp.

She married him, another ex-wife fuming around town. I heard the rumors from other friends, the ones about women not feeling safe around her, the hard-set jaw when she wanted something. Every day, sometimes twice a day, she called with updates on their affair until he left his wife and married her.

She had another baby; I had my first and only. And always, during this time, she showered me with gifts. Would you like a bunch of the sweaters my mother just sent?"

Of course I would; it snowed where I lived. But they never arrived, and I never asked. I couldn't—too much want that I didn't know how to disguise in my voice. The next time she promised something that never arrived, I braved it. "Hey," I said, "the box never arrived. Oh, she said, it slipped my mind. I'll have my assistant send it off today.

Snapshot:

This is a photo of The Box. The one she'd send me filled with the overflow from her closet, fabrics that said dry clean only and new towels with an astronomical thread count. This is the box I'd fill with my meager items and send back to her, hoping my offerings pleased. This box made dozens of trips back and forth; by the time it had to be retired, it was held together with shipping tape and colorful stickers.

Her marriage wasn't working out. Why wouldn't he do the simplest things around the house? Why didn't his kids like her? "Em," I'd plead. "Find a therapist. Work some of this shit out." But instead, the phone calls increased—two or three times a day now, and because of the time difference, often during dinner time. "Must you?" My husband would say, and I'd shrug and roll my eyes.

Sometimes now I wonder why I couldn't set a boundary, but really, I know why: I loved her. Our lives had been braided together over the years, forged in blood, bound by the secrets we shared.

Snapshot:

This is a picture of my front door, where I waited for the UPS truck that delivered The Box. My mother sent me two winter coats; do you need one? Of course I did. A wool coat was exactly what I needed. I waited for it to arrive —waited and waited some more. And when it didn't, I was too consumed with shame to ask, too undone by my need, too triggered back into my childhood with a punishing, withholding mother.

She divorced her husband and began an affair with a married man whose wife was slowly dying from melanoma. "Jesus," my husband said, "she's running amok." And she was —spinning out into her own world where no matter how many times we talked on the phone, I couldn't reach her.

"Honestly," I'd say, "I really think this has something to do with your father." Long silence. Em? Are you there?

She'd be crying, saying, "Yes, I probably need therapy." But then his wife died, and she married him, bought a fabulous redwood estate and dragged her three kids into another drama that seemed cruel and heartless, the makings of a story for the tabloids.

She ordered a bathing suit from Victoria's Secret but didn't like it. Would I? Yes. Open mouth bite down on hook.

Yes, I'd like it! But it never came. An extra pair of Ray-Ban sunglasses? Yes! They came. Sundresses? They never arrived. It was a hot summer, and did I need any silk blouses? They came. I felt like a rat in an intermittent rewards experiment. I grew lethargic, angry, and passive-aggressive. I didn't return her phone calls when she left desperate messages, pleading for advice. I started getting stoned whenever we did speak, trying to stop giving a shit, to stop imploring her to get some therapy, so that she might find some peace and leave a few decent marriages intact.

She divorced her husband and quickly met a man who everyone in America and beyond knew as The Cereal King, that's how familiar his name was. He was married with grown children, heir to a Midas fortune. I tried one more time. I wrote her a letter begging her to see a therapist before she broke up another marriage.

Snapshot:

This is the restaurant where we saw each other for the last time. We dressed up like we used to, tight dresses, cleavage, high heels, all the fun, sexy, girly things I loved about being her friend. We drank scotch on the rocks out on the patio, watching the waves crash. We tried. I tried. Where to begin? How to end? I was tired of her, tired of the futile hours on the phone while she justified the latest divorce and subsequent affair—the bitter ex-wives and the kids dragged from childhood into her chaos. But really, I was tired of the passive-aggressive games we were playing: dodging her phone calls and Em using all the glitter and glamour of her money to hurt me, the too too many of everything she offered so freely with an open hand, then pulled away just as

I was reaching for it. I was in therapy by now, working my ass off to get free of my mother and all my unmet needs, and that meant getting free of Em as well. Over brandy, she said that the hardest thing about having so much money was that everyone wanted some of it. Over brandy, what I didn't say was the hardest thing was having a friend with money and wanting some of it. But maybe that's exactly what she knew all along.

Snapshot:

This is the pair of earrings Emma gave me early in our friendship: double gold hearts, hers and mine. It's been twelve years since we've seen each other. She asked me to come to her wedding to the Cereal King and said she'd send me the tickets. I declined.

Sometimes, in a nostalgic mood, I'll google her and see what they are up to—lots of travel. They've developed a workshop that advises couples on how to sustain a meaningful marriage. She finally changed her last name from her father's to his, which I guess now makes her the Cereal Queen.

Sometimes I wear the double heart earrings. I put them on and take a moment to remember. Not so much the hard stuff at the end but all the fun: slathered in mud in Calistoga, Big Sur, endless joints, and scotches and Shermans smoked on her front porch. Endless secrets told when the light of the moon bounced off the water, and the stars shone clear. Remembering *the box* before it became an instrument of punishment. I put the earrings on and look at myself in the mirror. I've aged, of course, and she is the only one I want to talk to about it. How hard it is to let go of our youth and beauty; what it's like to have our gorgeous breasts sag from nursing and age. Should we consider plastic surgery? But of course, I don't call or write. We are way beyond that now. So, for a day, I wear my double gold hearts, and every time I see my reflection, I stop and remember her, stop and take a breath. I whisper, "Oh, Em."

9

THE BITE

JANET GARBER

For four decades, Helene was my best buddy. We stuffed socks under our shirts to see how we might "develop." She knew exactly what happened on that hitchhiking trip out to Colorado. She witnessed my humiliation by that snotty high-school sorority and bought me my favorite jellybeans. She understood my crush on the social studies teacher and why I was too afraid to even look at the cute boy in Bio. We held each other's secrets and told each other everything, until we couldn't.

Helene was not *the* popular girl in junior high school, but she had a bit of a following. As her "best friend," I decided I must be okay. She gave me an alternate worldview that pulled me away from familial dysfunction and out of the trough of teenage despair. We spent hours pretending to study physics, speaking bad French to her Alsatian father, and munching her crazy mother's deliciously burnt tollhouse cookies. Impulsively I wrote "Till death do us part" in her

JHS autograph book. Somewhat mortified, I realized I had given myself away. But I knew she had saved my life. And why couldn't we be friends forever?

Summers, I sent long letters to her in sleepaway camp or Europe, missing her terribly, confined, on those hot days before my family got air conditioning. Trudging back and forth to the library with ten or so books, reading Owen Wister's *The Virginian* or Booth Tarkington's *Alice Adams*—in short, checking-out anything big and chunky that would take a long time to get through. I always hated for a book to end, for a world unlike mine (my parents, younger brothers and I crowded into a small garden apartment, with me sleeping in the living room) to disappear.

In college and later, we went our separate ways. First, I stayed close to home and she went upstate. Then I engineered a great escape to Mexico and France, returning eight years later with my divorce in one hand and my two-year-old half-French baby in the other.

We were on different wavelengths then. She, the single Manhattanite, dining out at different ethnic restaurants every night, throwing parties for her fellow therapists, but not understanding that I couldn't afford a babysitter to attend. Though we saw each other infrequently, we always knew we were there: a piece of breathing history and memory, a witness. Most importantly, we could always start talking, finish each other's sentences, and skip from subject to subject in a slightly schizophrenic Queens, NY, way that made everyone else in the world dizzy. And always, we understood each other.

I probably liked talking to Helene more than I liked

talking to anyone else in the world. My mother, jealous, would try to bust into our sessions. We'd run off as soon as we could, close her out of our circle so we could continue our laughing and mischief and chatter, so meaningless to others.

Who else have I ever sat with for hours on end, engaged in nothing but conversation?

I know I loved Helene—she was the first person I ever loved. She showed me it was possible. She approved of me. We were the sisters we didn't have—bonded like cement.

Or so I thought. Here's what happened in December 1993, a ridiculous event, a slight thing maybe, a momentary lapse. Was it just an accident? Was it more? Helene's big black dog lunged at me as I stood talking to her in her Upper West Side apartment, biting me hard in the stomach, puncturing the skin. We had just returned from an evening celebrating her birthday; I was spending the night in the city at her place. We'd had a glass of wine each. I was waving my arms around, talking animatedly to her and her boyfriend about the film we'd seen.

ARGHH! The bite.

Stunned, I pulled down the waistband of my stretch pants to view the damage. The boyfriend pooh-poohed the whole incident, explaining that Blackie was protecting Helene; he refused to lock the dog up for the night. Quivering, I was forced to maneuver past Blackie to reach the bathroom. Helene dabbed some disinfectant on my wounds. I would need medical attention, which I sought out the next day—tetanus shot and antibiotics, a month to feel better and for the large purple bruises to fade away. And much longer for the other wounds.

Forgivable? Probably—until I learned I was not the only victim, that Blackie, with no provocation, had recently bitten *three* other people. Did Helene lock him up when people were around, muzzle him, or warn her guests? No, she took him off his leash the very next morning and let him run free in Riverside Park.

"It's nothing, Janet. I know you're going to make a big thing of it and worry. It's nothing."

"I hope this doesn't mean I have to lock up my dog every time you're over?"

"What do you want me to do, kill my dog?"

Helene never called to find out how I was doing. She acted put out when I asked her to reconfirm with the vet that Blackie had all his shots. Her only worry—that I'd report her to animal protection services or the department of health.

When I told a mutual friend what had happened, she responded, "But that's Helene. She's always been like that."

Maybe I needed Helene too much to see it. Hadn't she ditched my wedding because she didn't feel like coming back to New York from Michigan two weekends in the same month? She couldn't understand why I wouldn't pick some other date. She was the person I thought I knew best in the world, but I didn't.

Weeks later, I put all my pain into a letter. Could I scare her into taking action before someone else got chewed on? She had told me another friend, Sheila, would be visiting with her young son. Little children have such small fingers. I threatened to report the incident to the authorities.

Helene asked, "Why are you so cold?"

I was hurt. I was furious.

We had no contact for seven years. I wanted to forgive Helene though my therapist labelled her a "barracuda." I dreamt more than once of encountering her unexpectedly, perhaps in a park, and starting a casual conversation, saying to her, "Let's never discuss IT. Let's go on from here."

For seven years, I had a pain in my gut. I couldn't help myself. I missed Helene in my life.

January 2001. I sent Helene a postcard announcing the publication of my first book. Coy, she emailed, asking, "Is this *my* Janet Garber?"

We forged an internet connection and gradually began meeting and catching up. She met my new husband. She told me about her mother's passing, and she marveled at all the changes in my life. I could feel the tugs of that old comforting friendship.

I admit I kept a certain emotional distance. She seemed always to want more. When could we next meet? Could I sleep over at her apartment? Why not plan a weekend together?

Our roles had reversed.

Today, Helene and I, and another old friend get together periodically with our men to see Broadway plays, go to exhibits, and eat dinner. Helene and I meet for lunch a few times a year to exchange stories of our latest travels and travails.

Occasionally we start jabbering nonstop. I have the feeling at lunch's ending that there is still so much more to discuss. Gone are the days, the afternoons, when we could just lounge around our parents' homes, banging on her piano and singing tunelessly, making silly prank calls to boys we liked, speculating about our futures, and just talkingtalkingtalking. We say goodbye with air kisses and nary a look backwards. We never discuss IT. Perhaps we are not willing to gamble that our relationship can withstand this conflict; perhaps our friendship is both precious and fragile. We know better than to bring IT out and examine it in the light.

Will I ever trust her in the same way again? Never. But I think I understand her better now, who she is, who I am, both imperfect. She's not the person I needed her to be years ago. Not my champion. But I'm no longer the tentative adolescent in search of a champion.

I am happy to have Helene back in my life, even playing in a minor role. This smaller version of friendship still honors our shared past. The need to preserve our relationship calls to me, and if I haven't seen or spoken to her in too long a time, I feel anticipatory twinges of remembered loss. I'm called to value and preserve that long stretch of friendship that could never be reconstructed.

10

ACROSS THE WAY

BY P. F. WITTE

As children we were told never to go there.

i

But that day, years later, we both wound up at the same place; I, having just stepped off the bus, in full view of the abandoned lot, in full view of the body bag.

ii

• • •

Above the altar, the small circle of stained glass beckoned, the only piece of stained glass in that white clapboard church. Its image: Jesus with his arms opened wide, inviting us to him. And we below the stained-glass image of Christ, two young girls in burgundy choir robes, singing in soprano voices; Sunday mornings, April and I in the junior choir.

I don't believe either of us understood much of it; I don't believe we were able to take in our experience at church on a very deep, spiritual level. We were in church because our parents sent us, an insurance policy to guard the fact that we would grow up to be "good girls," that whatever our parents overlooked in our development from children into young adults, would surely be taken care of by God or Jesus Christ —whomever came to our rescue first.

Choir practice: April always arrived late but did what was expected, the whole time the look on her face during practice—the mouth hung in a half smile, a sort of did-as-she-was-told expression. At other times revealing yet another look, a look of restlessness, a look that held me: a wanting to escape, mixed with a trace of desire, what that desire was I wasn't all together sure of at that age.

That's how I knew her, a distant friend. But, in our circle, I was closer to her than most.

iii

The talk in the neighborhood about April, at fourteen: her boyfriends, her parents having little control over her, coming and going whenever she pleased. At sixteen, the rumors started changing: her runs to the city and something to do with drugs.

Sometimes we'd come across one another in passing (the bus stop just up the corner from the abandoned lot), I on my way home from school in the late afternoon, and April just starting her day off in the city. Once on the bus on the way home from college, trying to squeeze past the crowd of passengers, to get off at the next stop, I spotted April from the window, waiting to board as the bus slowed to the curb. There she stood, taking the last drag on a cigarette before tossing the rest of it in the street, wearing silver platform shoes, a miniskirt, neck and arms loaded with beads and bracelets, her blonde, wind-blown hair almost touching her waist.

Carrying an armful of textbooks, I push through the crowded bus to get off at my stop as she impatiently pushes her way in. As we pass one another in the crowd, almost touching in that impersonal way as passengers do, we simply nod at one another, and keep to our appointed destinations.

She was never one to talk, and I was never one to intrude on her firmly kept silence.

iv

April lived on a block in our neighborhood where there was an abandoned lot. I lived on a block where there was a dead-end sign, the swamp across the street, and across from that, the runway of Idlewilde Airport (today known as Kennedy).

The homes in that community were mostly beach houses that had once stood where the airport is now; beach houses set down on swampland that was filled in with ashes (the incinerated garbage of New York City). As the ash heaps settled, it caused the houses to slowly sink in lopsided fashion, front stoops and foundations sinking into the ground, as if they were being swallowed up by the very earth itself; here and there dotted with patches of land where marsh weeds grew, and small lots of land that no one ever thought of buying or claiming.

These images have stayed fixed in my mind for a lifetime.

v

That afternoon, like any other afternoon, the bus drops me off at the designated stop, I walk down the length of the block, see a crowd standing outside the lot, a bag being dragged out of the lot. I walk a few steps further, where April's house is located, parallel to the lot, notice the shade of the bay window rolled all the way up to reveal the action in the living room as a theater-goer might view the action on stage: her mother sitting on the living room sofa, her face in her hands, her children standing helpless before her, the police asking questions, jotting down notes.

I turn toward the bag. They're having trouble getting the bag out of the lot; it's caught on some branches. Then a voice from the crowd, "It's her; it's the Pell's kid." I turn to find the person who spoke, a man standing directly behind me. "What's going on?" I ask. "The Pell's kid," he motions toward the bag, and I notice the faint outline of a human body from within it, "...stabbed to death..." and then realize that it's April in that bag.

Some days I will tell you it was the "physical landscape," the weeds, the swamp, the lot, the airport across the way—that gave rise to our particular choices in life, to the decision that April chose, to the decision I chose, the paths we mapped out for ourselves.

Some days I will tell you that there were only two choices present in our community: the street or school. I could tell you that she came from a family of four, and therefore for a working class mother it was easier to raise two children as opposed to four, that perhaps she got lost somewhere among her brothers and sisters, that her mother's attention might have been needed for day-to-day survival.

And then again, I wonder: what experiences made us who we were? As far as April is concerned, I will tell you I haven't a clue. I can only tell you what was, from the distance where I stood then, and where I stand today.

vi

The facts as I know them: as five-year-old's, we were sent to church. We came together for a while, friends and voices in the church choir. As young women we chose vastly different paths. And circumstances and actions chose us. If we ran into one another, we'd exchange a nod of the head. I'd like to think this was our way of respecting our life choices, for better or worse, to give acknowledgment of our presence, our survival, and to let it go, or be, and that each of us, in our own way, was getting out.

PART IV

CORRESPONDENTS

My sister taught me how to write my name when I was about three. I remember writing my whole name: Jacqueline Amanda Woodson. I just loved the power of that, of being able to put a letter on the page and that letter meaning something.

—Jacqueline Woodson

11

DEAR ANNE

TAMRA WILSON

A couple of years ago, I received an unexpected email:

Dear Ms. Wilson,

I wanted to write and thank you for keeping the memory of my mother alive.

Tomorrow will be the 19th anniversary of her death and in a nostalgic moment I decided to Google her name to see what came up and came across your blog post.

To be honest I do not remember that phone conversation we had; I have had so many over the years with long-long friends of my mother's that it has almost become a normal part of my life, but reading your blog post touched me. Although my mother was only there for the first six years of my life, her life has shaped mine, and the friends she had shaped her; so by extension, you have shaped me also. I know I am the woman I am today because of her influence....

My father still has Mom's letters you sent us, and they are a treasured possession for both my sister and me. So, I just wanted to say thank you, it encourages me that my mother is remembered by people other than our immediate family, that she did not die to be completely forgotten.

It was signed simply, "Megan." We had spoken briefly on the phone once, as what might be seen as the final chapter of a friendship that began more than fifty years before, when my family moved to Tampa, Florida.

The year was 1961, and my parents were tired of harsh Midwestern winters. To their thinking, Davis Islands—a neighborhood in the middle of Tampa Bay—was the perfect escape. They rented a house across the street from a white bungalow with dark green shutters. That house belonged to the Halliburton family, and seven-year-old daughter Anne and I became fast friends. We had much in common. We were both brunettes and had brothers. We were born two weeks apart in August 1954. We both played the piano. Our families drove new Plymouths but, as I quickly came to realize, Anne inhabited a citified world. Her mother owned cocktail dresses. Her father was a banker and, if I remember correctly, a member of Ye Mystic Krewe of Gasparilla. One Saturday each year in early February, he dressed up as a pirate to ride the pirate ship to join a flotilla parading around Tampa Bay, launching a Mardi Gras-type festival—an activity my dad considered ridiculous.

Anne attended second grade at Seaborn Academy, a private day school for children on Davis Islands, while I rode a carpool to John W. Gorrie Elementary—the public school across the bridge that enrolled a number of Jewish children, some of whom were Cuban refugees.

Anne took dance lessons and sang about the Jelly Roll

Blues. We played Barbie dolls, Parcheesi and dress-up: she in her mother's fancy petticoat from Burdines and me in my mom's nylon half-slip from JC Penney.

My family adopted every neighborhood cat that would enter our door as Anne warned that we'd catch the cat-scratch fever, a silly notion for my mother who grew up with barn cats on the farm.

Anne and I usually played outside at her house because her yard wasn't full of sand burrs. One day we were amazed to see a large flatbed truck pull up in front of the Halliburton's house. The work crew proceeded to remove the entire front lawn and replace it by unfurling bright green rolls of sod. My parents shook their heads in amazement. Such strange people, these Floridians were.

After our winter in paradise, my mother decided that she felt less at home in Tampa than back in Shelby County, Illinois, and so my parents ended their lease and packed up the Plymouth.

Anne and I promised to write to one another, and sure enough, every few weeks, her letters arrived in our mailbox. "Dear Tammy, How are you? I am fine." Then, she would go on to tell me about her school, her friends, parties, swimming lessons, and what she had to eat at the club.

I would write back in kind, mentioning piano recitals, Brownie scout meetings and chicken dinner at Guy's Steak House.

Every Christmas and birthday, we exchanged cards and gifts. Some years it was stationery or dusting powder. One Christmas I received an envelope marked "Special Delivery" with a thirty-cent stamp—in the days when postage for an ordinary letter cost a nickel. Inside the precious envelope was a Christmas card, sent at the last minute by Anne, who had apparently forgotten to mail it, and she and her mother were horrified to discover the oversight.

There were times when I balked at writing to Anne. She seemed prissy and boy crazy and interested in her beach club, which sounded more glamorous than anything I was doing. But my mother insisted I keep writing. We had written this long, it would be a shame to let things go, and I sensed that her mother had told her the same thing. Moms tend to understand the pain of careless loss.

Some of Anne's high school letters contained sketches of clothes that her mother had bought for her. One mentioned a pin she received for her birthday that wasn't to Anne's liking. She might wear it "when I'm fortyish," she wrote.

Though a thousand miles separated us, we had a lot in common. We both majored in journalism at state universities —she in Florida, I in Missouri. We joined sororities, were interested in politics and within a year of one another, we married our sweethearts.

I visited Anne twice after we left Tampa, and she came to Illinois to cut the cake at our wedding. She was a lively, polished, and gifted young woman who landed a job for Sen. S. I. Hayakawa on Capitol Hill while I was working for the unglamorous Illinois Farm Bureau. Our parallel lives diverged further when she ran for the Virginia General Assembly in the 1980s. Then in her thirties, all signs pointed to a bright future.

Eventually we exchanged baby announcements and kept in touch until about 1989 when her letters mysteriously stopped. I tried coaxing her to write, first with a Christmas card that year, and a letter or two the next, but there was no response.

When the internet came along in the mid-1990s, I tried to locate her again. What was Anne doing now? Where was she? How could someone who had written to me all those years simply disappear without a word? True, we were both busy working mothers, but I missed her.

I should have picked up the telephone. Maybe I was too busy to do that. Or maybe I'd grown weary after twenty-five years of correspondence. I probably feared that she had grown tired of me too.

Then in July 2013, I made one more effort to find Anne. I Googled various forms of her name and places I knew where she'd lived. Surprisingly, I found her on Ancestry.-com. Apparently, she was still near Washington, DC, right where our correspondence had left off. So, I was certain that my cards and letters had reached her. I was thrilled to have the confirmation of her mailing address, again. And so, I wrote one more letter.

Dear Anne,

It's been a long time! I think about 25 years ago we lost track of one another. Recently I got on Ancestry.com and was able to locate your address. I often think of the time my family spent in Tampa and how we got to know one another. We must've been pen pals for 20 years or more.

I'd love to reconnect and see what you're doing these days.

We're in Western North Carolina. I'm part-time with the county library, and I'm still writing and published a story collection a couple years ago, "Dining with Robert Redford." I'm also a contributor to WFAEats, the food blog for the Charlotte NPR station. Do you still write as well?

I believe that you have a daughter who ought to be in her mid-20s? Our son is 27 and has been out West for three years now. He's something of a free spirit and enjoys Southern California. Ah to be young again!

Drop me a line if you get a chance.

Here's our email.

Hope to hear from you.

Love,

Tammy

Two days later our answering machine was blinking with a message from a young woman named Megan who said she had some information about her mother. I knew this couldn't be good. Hesitantly, I called the number. Anne had died of ovarian cancer in 1997, when Megan was only six—a year younger than her mother and I were when we began our long correspondence. Megan's father had raised the two girls, alone.

Megan's story grew even sadder. Anne's brother was also deceased, as were their parents. I mourned their loss though I hadn't heard from them in many years. They represented a part of my past that was now forever erased. Why did a young woman with so much promise, have to die so young?

I wrote to Anne's family, enclosing some letters she had written in high school and college. I found some photographs and mailed those too. This was one gift I could give that no one else could. And so, these old letters became a way for Anne's daughters to meet their mother as a young woman.

And for the first time in my life, I fully realized how wrong it was for me to resent growing older. I was about to turn sixty, a milestone many people resent. Yet, I now realized that I'd been given eighteen more years of life that Anne never had. Through no cause of my own, I'd been given the privilege of seeing my son grow up and experiencing so many things that Anne had not.

It so happened that I'd been asked as a lay person to deliver a sermon at church three days after my sixtieth birthday—two weeks after Anne would have turned sixty. And so, she became my sermon.

I began work by listing some things that I would want to tell my younger self, the me who used to write letters to the neighbor girl in Florida. Here's what I came up with:

Use your time wisely. You never know when it will run out.

Don't put things off. You may never get another chance.

Bad things happen; so do miracles.

Stay in touch. Keep writing letters.

Live thankfully. You did nothing to deserve the time you've been given.

Remember that life isn't fair; so, live it gracefully.

On August 14, 2014, we threw a birthday party for a houseful of friends. Anne would have liked it. The following Sunday, I delivered my sermon. I should have let Anne's family know, but I didn't get around to it until the internet did it for me.

On the 19th anniversary of her mother's death, Megan contacted me by email. She had come across the blog post about my "Anne sermon" and it had touched her, she said.

I'd kept Anne's letters. They were a part of me that I couldn't let go. I realized that those letters were a physical manifestation of a real person and an enduring friendship. Anne's words still live on those pages. I can feel her there. Anne's daughters can too. After all these years—our friendship, marinated in time and letters, endures.

Previously published in abbreviated form in a column published March 28, 2016 by the *Hickory Daily Record* Hickory, NC and the *Observer-News-Enterprise*, Newton, NC.

12

LITTLE BLACK MARKS

KATHLEEN GERARD

A binder full of emails: three years' worth of pages with subject lines that remain vivid in my memory: *Off-Nights vs. Nights Off; The Middle of The Middle Ages; A Sunshine State; I've had it — Moving to Australia; Thai Green Curry on Saturday Night; Word to the Wise Keep — Away from Hornets' Nests; Help! Camel's Back Near Breaking; March Forth on March Fourth...* I know exactly where I keep this binder in the basement.

I remember the day I met Cindy. I was to lead a spiritual writing workshop about journaling. I arrived at the meeting room early and saw her sitting alone at a table in an empty, darkened classroom. This woman was obviously as prematurely punctual as I.

"So, what's a girl to do to find a cup of coffee around here?" I asked, flipping on the lights and walking over to where Cindy was seated. I set my things down, put out my hand, and introduced myself. It wasn't like me to be so forward. By my very nature, I'm morbidly shy and reserved (I would later learn that Cindy was, too), but maybe caffeine withdrawal caused a mild form of extroversion to get the better of me that morning—or maybe it was providence.

When I suggested to Cindy that we go for a cup of coffee together, she agreed. We chatted for a while about writing and journal-keeping. She told me she was a graphic artist at a high-powered design firm in New York City, but on the cusp of middle-age, she felt she wanted more.

"Don't we all?" I said. "The problem is that people are often so busy living life, they don't have time to reflect upon it. Keeping a journal is a really good way to better understand yourself and whatever you're facing in life. And when you look back at what you've written, you can see how God has worked in your life. The crux is honesty—and to make time to practice the process."

". . . Of course, that's easier said than done," I later added, restating—during the workshop —what I'd already told Cindy. I offered that there was no right or wrong way to journal. The best I could teach were strategies on how to loosen up and use writing muscles unaccustomed to flexing. We hashed through some exercises that I'd hoped would remove barriers that kept people from being intimidated by the blank page. I thought it was a good session.

When the workshop ended, Cindy approached me and commented on how meaningful the exercises had been for her.

I was thrilled to know that I'd reached her.

"Any chance we might keep in touch?" she asked.

We exchanged business cards, and I didn't give it

another thought. How many times do people say, '*Let's do lunch,*' and it never happens?

You can imagine my surprise when Cindy e-mailed a few weeks later. She'd read some of the books on writing and journal-keeping that I'd suggested during the workshop, and she shared her thoughts. Unbeknownst to me (and maybe even to her, too), that was the start of an e-mail friendship that would continue to evolve for another three years.

We· were introverts who 'chatted' online about everything. Word by written word, we shared our thoughts about books, movies, food, recipes, restaurants, diets, and even our faith. Over time, I began to expect her e-mails—sometimes daily, sometimes weekly—and I looked forward to learning the latest news of her life and sharing about things we did, places and people we'd met, our work, and our aspirations.

Our correspondences built a bridge, and I discovered a kindred spirit. We were only a few years apart in age. Both small-town girls, we lived in the very same houses and towns where we grew up, just a little over an hour's drive from each other. We wrote about our siblings, our parents—our missing fathers from a young age. Memories: good and bad. Trips we'd taken and places we'd longed to visit. At that time, we were both single, without mates: childless, creative, striving, and searching. We commiserated about our love lives—the lack thereof and/or the horror stories of trying to meet and connect with new people and our trepidation of becoming lonely old spinsters and caving to cat-lady clichés.

We cheered ourselves out of ruts and promised to pray for each other. God and the challenges of our faith were at the center of our lives. And we viewed them through the prism of our Christian beliefs—and even our doubts. What great comfort I took in knowing another like-minded soul roamed this planet, sharing similar values and trying her best to get through this life—the mundane and the sublime —by relying upon a Higher Power.

Interacting online, we both admitted how, on some level, we were beginning to practice what we'd learned via our e-mail friendship—how to trust and be open again after some failed relationships, allowing ourselves to become vulnerable —out in the "real world." To this day, I'm convinced that because of Cindy's online presence in my life, I began to feel more comfortable in my own value and in turn with other people—and I gained confidence in my life and my work.

As our e-mail correspondences continued, Cindy mentioned how, as a graphic designer, she'd always considered herself a "visual person." Now, she felt that words were becoming more and more important to her.

"I'm a better writer and storyteller because of our e-mails," she wrote. "And I feel life is urging me to do more with my love of language. I'm just not sure what shape my writing should take."

I suggested she try her hand at writing a few essays. After she did, she asked me to read for her, and I did so, gladly. They were promising, encouraging starts.

A few months later, Cindy wrote and told me that she'd applied for a coveted creative-writing fellowship. When she was ultimately rejected, I empathized with the gravity of her disappointment and tried to explain how rejection is often par for the course. "It's lousy, but it's just part of the process built-in to a writer's life. If you stay in the game, your skin will thicken, and you'll get used to it."

But I sensed, from her counter-response, restlessness and impatience. She seemed unable—and unwilling—to grasp the concept of *being* a writer and the challenging and solitary nature of the task.

"A writer writes, so just keep on writing," I told her. "Your faith will show and guide you to what's next." It sounded like a platitude, but sometimes, that's all we can truthfully offer.

A few weeks later, a door finally opened for Cindy. She was asked to write a sermon for her church. I was thrilled for her and gladly championed the written installments of her transformation. It was as though she had found the missing piece to a puzzle that made the picture of her life now abundantly clear.

One sermon became two, then three and onward. She shared them all with me, and I read each with keen interest —moved and inspired. It was obvious that Cindy had a gift. But I sensed that things were suddenly changing between us. Cindy's correspondences began to wane, and when she did finally write, her e-mails were kept short and sweet. I kept on responding to her as though nothing were different until a niggling inside convinced me to take my cue from her and maintain the gap she was putting between us. I'd be lying if I said I didn't miss hearing from her regularly, but I had lived long enough to know that in any relationship there is always one person who needs and values the other a little bit more. The shift is often subtle and can fluctuate, like the tides. At the beginning of our friendship, I think

Cindy was the person who valued me more; the roles had reversed.

For the first time in three years, I took to my own journal in earnest. And by doing so, I began to question the measure of our friendship. Cindy and I—were we really friends? Could I really call us that? After all, what was it we really shared all those years—outside of written words? And what did those words really mean beyond mere thoughts that triggered our fingers to strike upon our computer keyboards? Were we just giving shape and form to our existence by typing little black marks on a computer screen, pressing 'send' and flinging the details of our lives and longings into the ephemera of cyberspace? I mean, did we know each other—really *know* each other—or were we just writing and existing in a vacuum?

Amid our dwindling e-mails, I was diagnosed with cancer. Mired in decisions and grappling with my fate, I wasn't sure if I should write and tell Cindy. The change in our relationship was palpable. After much deliberation, I decided that I shouldn't tell her. Cindy's e-mails had indicated that she was getting on with her life, moving in a new direction—and rightfully so. Therefore, I kept things between us as they were. I wrote to her only after she felt compelled to write to me, and I decided that I'd keep my side of things sunny and upbeat.

Yet, I was torn. Even though our friendship existed solely in cyberspace, I had come to consider Cindy one of the caring, dear friends of my life. And facing my cancer— the arduous physical and emotional challenge—I felt a need to turn to her. Maybe it was our shared spirituality? Our mutual passion for expressing our feelings via the written word? Whatever that indefinable something was, I felt a bond and wanted to talk to Cindy face-to-face—so I took a leap.

"I don't know why this hasn't come up before. I mean, we live fairly close," I wrote. "But after three years, aren't we overdue to meet for lunch—maybe we could even have breakfast or just a cup of coffee together?"

No response.

A week.

A month.

Two months.

The line between us went completely silent. The bridge was out, and I started to second-guess things. *Maybe I shouldn't have asked Cindy to meet? Maybe I've ruined a good thing? But if a relationship is to deepen and grow, doesn't it need to be stretched?*

Three months later, Cindy e-mailed a litany proclaiming how busy she was. I expected as much, but I never imagined that she wouldn't address my proposition—make an excuse or even decline the invitation. Instead, she simply wrote around what I'd asked as though enough time had passed for me to have forgotten.

But I hadn't forgotten. And I took her response—namely the things she didn't say—as confirmation to stop writing to her. I believed Cindy was sending a message imbued between the lines. Some bridges in our lives, perhaps, only run one-way. You can't make a U-turn and go back.

I believed it was time for me to move on.

Eighteen months later—after successful surgery and

treatment, along with a few prizes and awards for my writing—I logged in online, surprised to find an e-mail from Cindy waiting in my computer inbox. At first sight of it, my heart skipped. It had been such a long time since I'd seen her e-mail address, and for a moment, I just sat there, staring at the computer screen. The subject line read a simple, "Hello."

I didn't open the e-mail right away. Part of me was weighing the past, afraid to step back through that portal in time and re-live all those feelings of emptiness and loss I thought I'd put to rest. It was autumn, and I remember sitting back in my desk chair—looking past the computer screen and out the nearby window. Red and golden leaves sailed toward earth, landing without a sound. The suspense of first discovering that email was short-lived; I hit the 'read' button and revealed a screen full of apologies for Cindy's absence. She went on, detailing how she had left her high-powered job as a graphic artist in New York City and was currently enrolled, studying at Yale Divinity School to become a Minister.

She wrote, "It's amazing how I'm finally combining my love for words and spirituality in such a fulfilling way." I could tell from her tone that she was rejoicing in having found her path and purpose.

"And you—how are you?" was the last line of her e-mail. "I hope we can pick up right where we left off."

Cindy was obviously thriving, and I felt joy and relief in the discovery of how things had shaped up for her. In the time that had passed and in the distance that had come between us, we had both forged ahead and had grown. In my response to her, I conveyed those feelings enthusiastically then briefly filled her in on the good news, only the good news, of my life.

Once again, I hit 'send.'

And that was it.

She never responded after that.

It's now been eight years since I heard from Cindy. I still remember her in my prayers every day and with special intent each Christmas and on her birthday. That will never change.

I've printed and saved all of our emails. They're kept in a thick binder in my basement. I haven't made time to read them all, and I doubt I ever will. But the trove of those letters, and my knowing exactly where to find them, offers a visceral slice of my history with an actual rather than virtual friend. She was a valued presence in my life that helped me to grow. And for a little while at least, those little black marks—however transient and fleeting—fulfilled some sort of need in each of us.

PART V

HERE'S THE THING

We have woven a web, you and I, attached to this world but a separate world of our own invention.

—John Keats

13

TWO KINDS OF GARDENERS

BETSY ROBINSON

An urban landscape designer I know says there are two kinds of gardeners: the coddlers and the pragmatists. My sick ward of houseplants rescued from New York City garbage cans inspired her remark. She specializes in high-rise terraces and exquisite window boxes in brownstone front windows. She places a high priority on the right look; if a plant doesn't perform, she chucks it.

For years, I was a plant killer. I had good intentions but forgot to water. I gave up buying plants because I knew they'd end up in the trash. Then my mother died, and I did a 180. Not only did I water the plants that I inherited from her, but I bought grow lights and three kinds of plant food. Inspired by my new lush indoor garden, I soon became a plant rescuer, pulling leggy geraniums and discarded amaryllis bulbs out of dumpsters and nursing them back to health. I will not give up on anything until it proves that it's unequivocally dead. I am a coddler.

"It's junk," says my best friend and neighbor "Angie" as I stare, incredulous, at the crushed remains of the large leafy impatiens she's yanked from her window box. "It stopped flowering. It's dead." Angie is a pragmatist.

"It was resting!" I retort, pulling the mutilated plant out of our garbage. "Everything needs to take rests."

"It's junk," repeats Angie, continuing to tidy her boxes.

"It is a living thing."

Angie looks at me like I'm crazy, but when she sees my distress, her eyes soften.

"You value nothing!" I explode. Then I turn my back and leave, full of self-righteous sadness that lasts the four flights to my apartment.

Why am I so upset? Why do I get into these stupid arguments? Angie's been my best friend for many years. She's a beautiful woman who tends to only see her flaws. She works in the fashion industry, and it's her job to make things look good. From my vantage, seeing that plant in the garbage was like seeing her throw herself away. The next day, I apologize and try to explain. She listens. Her eyes get wet, but she doesn't cry.

Many months later, Angie asks me to cat-sit when she goes on vacation. I'm used to seeing new plants every time I enter her apartment. She buys without inquiring about growing conditions, throws out, then buys some more. The only constant is a dracaena she's had since college when she took a cutting from a plant at her restaurant job. She keeps it drenched, yet it never gets root rot. It thrives in the dark of this ground-floor apartment with apparently no light requirements. I am watering the new azalea and dieffenbachia when I notice an old friend—a now bushy, deep-green aglaonema that I rescued from a West 71st Street garbage can and presented to her a couple of years ago. The last time I saw it, it was a couple of anemic-looking leaves. I was sure Angie kept it only to keep from offending me. And now, it is flowering. The white-spathe blooms, scattered though the plant as if professionally arranged, resemble those of the peace-lily—so lovely that I well up.

I am very quick to judge: Right is right, and wrong is wrong. Angie was wrong to throw out that impatiens. I am right to rescue living things that others discard. I'm good. She's bad.

But her aglaonema is flowering. They rarely flower, and certainly not in ground-floor city apartments with dry heat and no sunlight.

I recall my anger at Angie. I recall the look in her eyes when I apologized and explained.

Her aglaonema blooms.

Maybe wrong was right. Maybe she had to discard the impatiens, and we had to have that awful conversation for us to hear ourselves. Maybe it all happened in just the right order for her to grow, to want to nurture the abandoned little plant … and for me to see it, to be stunned enough to see that I was wrong to think I was so right. And how magnificent it is to get to learn it this way from the lush and flowering aglaonema that grows with care in an imperfect place.

14

COLLECTING

LEAH ANGSTMAN

W hen my first best friend died in a car accident of which I still can't openly speak to this day, I began collecting those little ceramic Wade Whimsies figurines that come in Red Rose Tea boxes. My mother was absent, overseas somewhere, and my father— the sort to slice into a block of Spam and call it dinner— wasn't the best confidant for a grieving teenager. His only sibling had died when he was in his thirties, and I didn't hear the name pass his lips but what could be counted on a single hand. I was alone with Dad's Spam and a fistful of ceramic miniatures I'd found in an attic box.

At first, I only collected them on the good days—the days I spent ten minutes without thinking of Chris' lifeless body, or his shattered head going through the passenger window, or the way he broke apart in our hands as we waited for the ambulance.

The good days began, ten minutes at a time. And if I

went the full ten minutes, then I rewarded myself with a walk down to the antiques district on the other side of the railroad tracks to barter something for a Wade figurine in the "cheap bin." It'd be years before I'd paw through the actual antique selection with my forklift-operator-in-local-warehouse paychecks, but as a gateway drug, I was content with the cheap bin of innumerable replicates and ugly, botched paint jobs.

Because we were young when Chris died, we mourning students were easy to gather for a memorial. Carrying a ceramic raccoon from the Animals II Series, I walked from my house to the church where his casket was closed, next to the piano at which I would have to play and sing wrenching songs like "Tears in Heaven" and Sarah McLachlan's "I Will Remember You." How we choir kids could manage to do this to ourselves, I'll never quite comprehend. I even delivered a eulogy full of inside jokes to disparate audience cliques, to make people forget their pain for a minute and laugh, and I managed not to crack until the very end. But there was something false in all of it, too. He was *my* best friend; he wasn't *their* best friend. And yet, there they all were—people who'd hardly known him, playing a grief card I just couldn't imagine was really in their hands to play.

Wade Whimsies are not adorable objects. They come from a cheaply-made mold and are churned out by the thousands in an industrial kiln, and then smothered in a grossly uneven pottery glaze. Most of them are animals, stamped on the butt with a tiny, somewhat indistinguishable *WADE*. In 1967, the Canadian tea company, Red Rose, began putting the famous English miniatures in their tea boxes as free premiums at a time when that was fashionable in the food and beverage industry. I can't even tell what some of the animals are, and others look to be recycled from earlier sets with merely a different glaze color. The Canadian sets are always glazed prettier than the American sets and are harder to find, while the 1970s Canadian Nursery Rhyme Series go for a small fortune. I can't say for sure what it was with these miniatures that triggered my interest. It could have been that, once you have two of something and realize that more exist, there is a secret joy in the "X"s of a treasure map —the pieces, the clues, and a chest full of something desirable and valuable at the end.

I somehow found my way into someone's car in the long processional—always so long for young people—placed like a limp doll in the front seat by a person kinder than I felt, staring through the windshield at the little orange funeral flag on the antenna. I think I was numb, but I remember silly things: congratulating myself on not crying, spots of dirt on my new shoes, wondering what the afterparty might have for food because I wasn't getting enough to eat with Mom gone. It was the summer I stopped eating, the summer I stopped doing everything, living, breathing, telling any truths. It was the summer I stopped answering questions, combing my hair, wearing clothes that fit, coming home at a reasonable hour, coming home at all. Beyond the funeral flag, the mound of dirt looked enormous when we pulled up to the site. He was only a boy—did they know he was only a boy?

Now, when I see this scene, I can see it for the idyllic Midwestern countryside it is. He's buried far off from the main drag, in a place where no dust kicks up, where cars must be destined specifically to traverse. Robins sing, and the summer heat is oppressive and muggy and full of mosquitoes, but the land is resilient, and the undulating land holds up well. The green remains, despite the sun's attempt to scorch it. There's an apple blossom in one corner that retains its blooms like winning a dare, and you can hardly see that paces away is another grave of a student we lost the following year to an equestrian accident. But on this day, back when I didn't notice these things, all I saw was Dee, draped over the resting coffin like a discarded stole, weeping in histrionics that I could hear from the car before I could see them. Dee, whom he didn't even like, leaned—wailing and clutching his coffin like a leech. I wanted to tear her from it and cast her into the hole, not least of which because I wished I'd had the bravery to toss myself across his casket. Had she even sat beside him in a class? Did she know his middle name? James. His middle name was James. His favorite color was blue, and he hated bananas. He was going to DePaul University. She didn't know. She didn't know him like I did. I, who'd figure-skated with him, danced with him in the rain, sent messages in bottles with him down Sycamore Creek, and walked arm-in-arm with him on the railroad tracks like some outtake from *Stand by Me*. Funeral goers patted her arms and cooed to her like mourning doves. Why didn't I have the courage to fall over his casket and let the dirt pile on top of me? Why did I feel such an urge to tell her he had never liked her, to ruin her wailing drama? And who was I to speak for the dead?

I was the dead myself. I was so desperate for any

communication from him that I made up his voice, as if I could speak for him. I congratulated myself again on not crying. I stroked the raccoon in my pocket, and I made it through the day. And then, for a while, I stopped making it.

Grief is a cunning thing. It eats into you in ways that feel so apart from your body that you don't really believe it's you who's feeling it. You think the problem lies with the outside world, and you're the only one who can see it, sense it, identify it for what it is. For the first month, I slept in Chris' room, curled up on his bed, listening to his Rage and Sinatra CDs and draping shirts from his closet over my face. His mother would bring me Red Rose Tea, and together we'd hunt for the figurine in the box. I remember promising her that I'd leave when I couldn't smell him any longer, and her love for me was so great that she held herself together like royalty, and even though I knew she was hurting, her grief was one more reality I couldn't see. For days and weeks and years, I was angry when I thought of his casket, tried to picture the harrowing day, the forced stillness, and could only conjure Dee's body sprawling, wailing, pounding her fists into his black box. By then, I had become useless to the world, a sour and sorry copy of myself who sat in my room and read books, didn't look up when anyone spoke to me, and got a hall pass for the counselor's office whenever I had a math test I didn't want to take. I was unbearable because someone else's grief could not possibly equal mine.

As with all collections, there are rules. We give ourselves parameters for what will make us happy. First, it was good days when I'd go the 10 minutes, then days when I was no longer afraid to attempt doing the things I'd once done with my best friend. When I first set foot on the ice with my figure-skates again, it was such a feat that I rewarded myself with three miniatures.

As my collection developed, so, too, did my rules. The desire to get the pieces from anywhere and anyone, by any means necessary, morphed into getting them only from the antiques district in my hometown, where hundreds could be found, but most were replicates, so my eye grew discerning. The current collection—the Circus Series at the time I started collecting, and the American Heritage Series at the time you're reading this now—could only come from the purchase of Red Rose Tea boxes at the store, and I'd beg my mother to buy two at a time. I'd pull one from the front of the shelf and one from the back, convinced my chances of getting different figurines decreased by their closer proximity to one another. Once eBay became a thing that people did, I made a new rule that I couldn't buy online. There are some expensive pieces available on antique sites that would complete my collections of each series in the span of a single mail delivery, but I cannot order them; I must *find* them. In this way, it is finding pieces of myself. It is the treasure map. And because of this stubborn hunt for all my pieces, I have most of the figurines from every individual series, Canadian and American, since 1967, but I still don't have a *single* complete series. Just as I'm learning that I will never be a complete person, I'm learning to be okay with never having a full set.

A few years later, I went with my brother to his first high-school reunion because he's one year, one month, and one day older than I am. We have a lot of mutual friends across our two consecutive grades. Chris would have been in my brother's graduating class had he lived to graduate, and also in his grade was Dee. When I saw her at the picnic, I felt meanness conquer my composure, as if—like on a day six years prior in a graveyard where she'd made a blubbering fool of herself—she didn't have any right to be there, either. I was in a circle of old friends, lamenting how wine coolers being free didn't make them taste any better, when she walked up to me. Conversation ceased, and the friends sensed a cue to disband until it was just the two of us.

She asked if I remembered Chris' funeral, and I tried not to make any guttural horse sounds. She told me a bully had once knocked her books from her hand, and Chris had picked them up. She told me she knew he didn't care for her like that, but she'd been in love with him since middle school. She told me she was jealous of my friendship with him, but that all changed the day of the funeral when she'd seen my stoic grief, when she'd been glad we'd had each other for our short time. She told me she'd been all right during the funeral, but that she lost it when my eulogy mentioned a drama club incident to which she'd been privy. She told me her cousin had died a week before Chris, all of us the same age, and she couldn't get it out of her mind, how close it had all been. She told me it was my eulogy that made her cry so violently at the gravesite, that she'd wanted him to come back, *for me*. For me. For me. Her grief had not been only for herself, as mine had been. Her cries had been for the others who were hurting.

That day ended in an embrace. Like the moment when Lizzy Bennet exclaims over Mr. Darcy's effusive letter, "Till

this moment, I never knew myself," I hadn't known who I was until someone else pointed it out. Dee never knew my past resentment toward her behavior, and I'm glad I kept that constitution, but knowing what was internalized still floors me— how blind a suffering person can be to the suffering of others. We like to assume our suffering would make us more compassionate creatures, but it can also make us stubborn and selfish and unbending. I wasn't truthful with my own pain and loneliness. Consequently, I couldn't be open to anyone else's. I had to let myself hurt, and I had to let others hurt. Forget the game of who could love the best, the most, and be loved the most in return; love is not a finite measure, and in claiming to be the only one with rights to feel it, I cheated others of their chance to love what I also loved, and cheated myself of the chance to partake in that shared love. Love that should have been celebratory, not competitive. I don't have a corner on grief. I don't even understand the thing, let alone make any claims to it. I only know that we all have to give space and permission for each to experience their grief as it comes. When I understood, I could drop my claims and join the community of those who love Chris.

My collection rules have changed since then. Now that it's been two decades and most days are good days, I don't reward myself for the happy thoughts anymore, or I'd have a hundred full collections a hundred times over. Instead, I reward myself for the grief and for my heartache at other people's grief. Through the towns and the miles and the years and the loves, I have learned—like Dee who'd been so much wiser before me—to feel strongly. My mother's cancer, my friend's cousin's overdose, a brother's divorce: grief comes at us in waves and is constantly changing, never complete, as cunning as ever. But on the days when I feel it —when I have to let them all feel it for themselves—I take myself down to the Saturday flea market and hunt and peck for the pieces that might eventually make me a complete set.

Previously published under a different title in *Nashville Review*, April 2019.

15

FLORENCE AND MARION

MARA BUCK

This is a tale of two baskets: twisted willow, flexible strands woven into strength; the strength is friendship. Baskets, now patinated by the touch of decades, that carry the resonance of Florence and Marion.

Her diary, leatherette, the color of fog, spine dingy and cracked, handwriting shaky on the lined pages, is safely somewhere, casually secreted there by me not so long ago. I have spent a day searching in usual and unusual places without success. Still, the book is small, like my grandmother and easily overlooked. She of the liquid eyes, too dark for polite society, the wavy hair coiled tightly against intrusive questions—an enigma, the person, Florence Ella Abbott Albee. Four feet ten inches, delicately sculpted from the clay of pure stubbornness, well below one hundred pounds, yet when her tiny feet were placed just so to her liking, no force in the known and unknown worlds could adjust her a fraction. She never bothered with much of anything for herself, a creature of few needs and fewer wants who crocheted handkerchief borders and scanned Readers' Digests and inexplicably became fascinated by boxing matches once we finally owned a television. A creature of habit and habitat. A nautilus.

Throughout those years of my remembering, she consented to leave the house only if driven directly to a restaurant or to the new W T Grant's outside town, where she made monthly purchases of plastic flowers when her widow's pension arrived, selecting seasonal colors and discarding them at whim. She never cared to learn to drive and, although in sturdy shape from a lifetime of housework, never walked beyond the perimeter of the lawn of the house in which she lived. Never. It failed to concern me as a child. The groceries were delivered, or I ran errands. Was she an agoraphobic long before such a disorder was ever considered? I never questioned. I was accustomed to strangeness.

Mrs. True brought, to the door, fifty-cent bouquets for my grandmother, and my grandmother paid her the fifty-cents for the phlox, zinnias, and snapdragons. At a time when fifty-cents was a pound of ground chuck and a loaf of bread, my grandmother bought a fifty-cents bouquet from Mrs. True every week of the growing season. Mrs. True grew the flowers on her farm outside the city, which was not really a city but a place where the roads crossed. I remember the woman's hands with spatulate fingers, hands veiny as the leaves of the zinnias, hands themselves tinted green from the constant contact with things that grew. I remember, I think. Or was Mrs. True the lady who nurtured violets in her basement and carried the plants to Florence, that same Mrs. True who had a son in later years, a good boy with Down syndrome, a nice man whose name I forget, whereabouts unknown. Was that Mrs. True?

Bouquets of petals and plastic and violets and fifty-cents and a nice boy-son and all long gone, only for me to remember and wonder *what good did it all bring, what lesson?* I want so much to remember, but really to what purpose? This was my grandmother. I'm sure Florence knew, and I wish I could ask her.

And occasionally, Marion would visit.

Since, in no way, is this an attempt at genealogy, I will pass along the stories in the tradition of rumors that were handed down to me. It was known that Marion and Verge immigrated to Maine from New Brunswick, and that Verge worked on the railroad. There were no children, and they lived by themselves, without relations, until the end in a white clapboard cape largely untouched by the twentieth century, heated with wood and coal. Marion cooked on a monstrous cast-iron wood stove with pots at the rear, keeping water hot for dishes and bathing. She pumped a treadle Singer in a racing rhythm, and hand-cranked a tub washer, squeezing out the stove-hot water through the wringer before bundling the spotless sheets outside to the clothesline that pulleyed across the backyard. Verge handled the wood-chopping, the coal-loading, and the snow-shoveling. They owned neither car nor television, and Verge listened to the radio or read the paper by kerosene lamp as he sat in the Empire mahogany rocker that I inherited—the rocker in which I sit, the rocker that soothes my back. On those quiet evenings, Marion would braid rugs from scraps of wool leftover from sewing the goodly portion of their clothes and some of mine. After supper, she set the table with the dishes for their pre-dawn breakfast, cups judiciously turned bottoms-up in their saucers. There must have been some electricity in the house because Verge's radio was a big wooden box of a thing with tubes inside that he would show me if I promised not to touch. He never believed in daylight savings time, harrumphing, "Gol-danged nuisance invented by the government to keep the working man's nose to the grindstone." Verge kept all the clocks in the house well-wound and oiled, and the hours that they struck were his hours, hours that never sprung ahead nor fell back. Of course, there was a telephone because Florence and Marion would talk on occasion, setting up the bare facts of an upcoming visit, spare conversations as if words were precious to be spent with utmost care, not unlike change to count and save for hard times to come.

As a pig-tailed grade-schooler, I sometimes spent the night with Marion and Verge. On these visits, I became a character in an old-fashioned book, snuggled under a handmade quilt in a carved oak bedstead that loomed around me with comforting shadows. The flickering of the Franklin grate in the fireplace kept me company. Nothing was amiss in that house; it was secure in ways I have not found since.

A gigantic flowering plant occupied a sunlit corner of the living room between Verge's rocker and the mantelpiece with the Seth Thomas clock. "That's a Christmas cactus, child," Marion said. "My mother had that up in Canada, and I brought it all the way here when we moved. 'Spect it must be already almost a hundred years old. Bright pink flowers like that every Christmas. Pretty thing."

I remember that plant blossoming only in the winter and so old and vibrant—magic to a child.

Marion cooked everything from scratch. Apples from their storm-bruised tree were simmered into wholesome sauce, elderberry bushes yielded jam, produce from traveling farmers became pickles sparkling in Mason jars, and the linoleum-shod kitchen breathed a constant yeasty haven of fresh baking. Yards of hand-pulled molasses taffy greeted trick o' treaters, and loaves of bread found their circuitous ways to Thanksgiving dinners for the needy. Her handknit mittens graced many tables at the church bazaars, and as regular as Verge's dependable clocks, every few days, she would overfill her willow basket with Snickerdoodles and fudge and march across the street to the hospital coffee shop with her donations. And just often enough, less so as the years passed, her basket crammed with still-warm cookies and elderberry jam, this stout woman, with ostomy bag hiding below her pioneer heart, would trudge a couple miles along the cracked sidewalks of the small city to visit her friend Florence.

My grandmother wore an afternoon dress whenever she received callers, customarily a solid shade, more somber than the floral cotton housedresses appropriate for morning chores. Marion would be similarly attired, both sporting cardigans despite the weather, both in sensible lace-up Red Cross or Natural Bridge shoes, stockings with straight seams, wedding bands, simple watches, and pearl button earrings their only jewelry. Florence brewed tea, which they each sipped plain in floral china cups, saucers balanced on demure laps, Marion's cookies resting respectfully on a familiar silver tray. They would each enjoy one—only one, with only one cup of tea.

I would burst in from school, say hello, grab a cookie, and run outside. I never knew what they discussed. I never heard them laugh or raise their voices. They were quiet, formal women, and theirs was a quiet formal friendship that lasted years longer than many of my raucous friendships.

When my father's mill shift ended, he would stick his head into the living room to nod a polite greeting. "I'll drive you home anytime you're ready, Marion. Just say the word." He would gobble a few cookies in the kitchen where he nursed instant coffee by himself until departure time—a formal play in one act whose participants and scenes varied only with the seasons. There was no hugging, no kissing, no joking, and no gossip—only the security of true and rare comradeship.

Upon prodding from my mother, Florence would allow herself to be driven to Marion's home for a return visit with her own basket piled with her own remarkable Toll House cookies. I was not privy to those visits, although I'm sure they were as formal and polite, and I'm equally sure Verge found busy work in the shed at those times. Invariably, Marion would slip some taffy or a doll dress or mittens into my grandmother's basket for the journey home to me.

What did they discuss, these two close friends, stout, energetic Marion and tiny, elusive Florence? The ladies of the corset and the cardigan, the hairpin, and the apron, who never revealed that which was not proper. Did they know passion, wish on the moon, have secrets? Did they speak of dreams undone, or was such talk unnecessary to them? And why do I ache to know it now?

Even before I left for college, the visits grew more sporadic, but in the manner of youth, I was more interested in my own blossoming life than in anyone else's, and I ceased to notice the elderly. Verge passed first, then Marion soon after, suddenly, I believe, at home. Did I ever know the details, did I not want to know, to selfishly cradle my memories of a secure place where the bread was fresh, and the clocks were wound, and the table was always set? These thoughts still gnaw at me.

Today, the gigantic spreading Christmas Cactus graces my kitchen as my one surviving family member, and an ethereal graphite drawing of Marion as a curly-headed Edwardian child stares from across the room. Sometimes, when the light is just right, the pink blooms of the plant are reflected in the wavy glass of the drawing and seem to cast a blush on Marion's cheeks. The plant blooms several times a year in my house. I think this is just as it should be.

Except for these personal treasures willed to me, the hospital was the beneficiary of Marion and Verge's estate. The house was abruptly torn down for a parking lot. It has been gone for years, and I still shudder as I drive by. Someone should have remembered the kindness of all those cookies and the kitchen that baked them. Some doctor should have moved in, but there were no stainless appliances, no granite counters, and no cable-ready conveniences. The ceilings were low, the windows were multi-paned, and the glass was irregular. The floorboards were worn, and there was only one bathroom with a clawfoot tub. Unlivable. A storybook house of comfort for two elderly people and a sometimes child, but not good enough for anyone else.

Our family home, Florence's and mine, was also plowed under for shiny vinyl commercialism. A huge chain drugstore—a temple of pharmaceuticals—grew on the site. Whenever I buy cough drops and pick up prescriptions, I stand in the same spot where the sun coursed through our living room windows, and I remember when the forsythia cast gold throughout that place where the ladies sipped their tea. And I marvel that I am here, and everything else is not. There are days when I would trade almost anything to see Marion's full basket on our dining room table.

To honor special occasions, probably birthdays, though I can't recall, I gave away the two willow baskets to those who had admired them. My childhood best friend, who munched my grandmother's Toll House cookies and whose name resides forever in that very diary, noted a lovely girl, now displays Florence's basket in her downstairs powder room, where it cradles magazines, the Reader's Digest among them. The effrontery of magazines in the bathroom would shock Florence, who never admitted to any bodily function. Marion's basket lives quite properly on an antique pine dresser in another friend's home, where it holds, appropriately, letters from friends. The baskets will never again meet, separated by a hundred miles or more, and I alone know exactly where they are. When I am gone, they will continue their wicker lives, perhaps move to other destinations, still employed for friendly purposes, but never by truer friends.

And just a few days past, when I read that cracked diary,

that book I have now misplaced, my grandmother's simple phrases chatting with no one about the weather and the fact that the folks had gone to the movies and said the show was just fine, in the midst of the weather and the bits and pieces of trivia that Florence felt it mindful to record, in that same casual style, she wrote, "They say that Marion died today. Don't know why."

Previously published in *Pithead Chapel Literary Journal*, Volume 2, Issue 10, 9/13.

PART VI

WHEN YOU'RE NOT HERE

Perhaps all the dragons in our lives are princesses who are only waiting to see us act, just once, with beauty and courage. Perhaps everything that frightens us is, in its deepest essence, something helpless that wants our love.

—Rainer Maria Rilke

16

SERIAL BESTIES

PATTY SOMLO

In my earliest memory, I am standing at the window, watching Hillary Sheehan's blue plastic swimming pool sail past. I don't remember anything else about Hillary Sheehan.

After the hurricane that lifted Hillary Sheehan's pool into the air and carried it past my watchful eyes, I left Andrews Air Force Base, Maryland, with my two older sisters, mom, and dad. I never saw Hillary Sheehan again. At the time, I didn't realize I was losing my best friend because I had never lost a best friend.

I have a black-and-white photograph of my third-grade class at Hickam Elementary School on the island of Oahu. As one of the shortest kids, I'm easy to find, smack in the center of the front row. My wide grin reveals a dark space where a tooth had recently loosened, and with a lot of jiggling, came out.

The other kids in the photograph look unfamiliar enough

to be strangers. I have trouble believing that not even one of those kids was my best friend, but it seems that way to me now.

The summer after that photograph was taken, we left Hawaii on a huge ship, the S.S. Matsonia. A few weeks later, we moved into a house in Mt. Holly, New Jersey, on a street that wasn't yet paved.

My childhood as a military kid went on like that, moving from place to place, though the pace of the moves quickened. From the time I entered the sixth grade until the tenth, every year, I started school in a new place. The names of two best friends stand out: DeeDee Malone and Carla Broome. DeeDee was blond and funny, and she was my best friend when we lived at Scott Air Force Base, Illinois.

Of all the best friends, I have the clearest memory of Carla Broome, who I palled around with in Germany. Carla spent hours every day washing her face because she had bad, oily skin. She used special soaps and lotions and covered her cheeks, forehead, and chin with rubbing alcohol and pimple cream. As much as I hate to say it, all the special treatments were in vain. Most of the time, she resorted to slathering liquid makeup on to hide the acne.

Carla was smart, funny, and tough. If it wasn't too cold, she wore a boxy black leather jacket. Otherwise, she had on what the rest of us did—a dark-colored wool Loden coat. These dull German jackets were practical and unflattering, with wooden buttons that looked like miniature beer barrels and deep hoods to protect us from the incessant rain and snow.

After Carla poured peroxide on her brunette hair, she

ended up with streaky dark-red highlights. My dirty-blond hair went platinum. Memory tells me it was Carla's idea for us to try our hand shoplifting in the downtown Frankfurt Woolworth's store. We only took small stuff —white lipstick, frosted pink nail polish, and *Evening in Paris* cologne. One day, we got caught.

The Woolworth's manager dragged us up the stairs to a dark office filled with metal file cabinets and piles of paper on the matching gray metal desk. He made a phone call on one of those huge black phones everybody had in Germany then. In minutes, the German police, the *Polizei*, arrived.

During the two years we lived in a dreary second-floor apartment at Rhein-Main Air Force Base, stuck in the woods about a half-hour's drive from Frankfurt, Germany, I saw Carla practically every day. Each weekday morning, I walked to her apartment to pick her up for school, and we would head over together to the parking lot in front of the base theater, the teen club, and the beauty shop to wait for the bus. No matter what time I got to her apartment, Carla would still be washing her face, a clear plastic shower cap holding back her hair.

I can't remember saying goodbye or feeling bad about leaving Carla or even missing her. In fact, I can't remember which of us left Germany first. I recollect that we didn't keep in touch. I don't have a clue what happened to Carla, and writing this, I realize I've never wondered about it before.

After Germany, we moved back to the little town in New Jersey, and my father went to Vietnam. During my junior year in high school, I had a hard time making friends. Most of the kids in town had known each other since kindergarten. I lived in a world apart, as if I were traveling through life in a layer of Cling Wrap. Activities and classes went on at school, and I observed, always from afar.

I spent a lot of time with my sister Carol, watching old black-and-white movies on our small TV, which sat on a metal stand at the end of our twin beds. The only reason we left the room on Saturday and Sunday afternoons was to use the bathroom or run downstairs to get more Coke. I began to count the days until I could leave home and go to college.

Finally, in early September, that day arrived. Walking behind my overweight mom, her puffy upper arms exposed in a sleeveless cotton dress, I must have looked like a poor refugee kid, struggling with my cardboard boxes, paper bags, and olive-green Samsonite suitcases. I had chosen The American University in Washington, D.C. because they had a good program in International Relations. Mostly, I hoped a degree in International Relations would give me a chance to travel.

AU, as the school was affectionately known, was an expensive private university that attracted the children of the rich, which I hadn't known before. Wealthy Jewish kids from the suburbs of Philadelphia, Chicago, Boston, and New York flocked to the place, and they were about to become my new friends.

The two women's dorms, Anderson Hall and Letts, faced one another across an open concrete area known as *The Quad*. There was an AU tradition I learned about only after having run the gauntlet. On move-in day every year, fraternity guys would gather alongside the steps and porches of the dorms to check out the new female crop. I don't remember what I had on. But I can picture our little entourage—my mom, my small-town brother-in-law, Everett, who everyone thought looked like Elvis, and my sister Barbara, her teased-up hair sprayed into an unmovable bouffant—looking like country bumpkins, next to the other students and their tan parents in designer duds, showing off great figures from hours of tennis.

My newest best friend, Alice, lived in Anderson, a few doors down the hall from my room. By spring break, we'd become close enough for Alice to invite me home.

Alice had clear pale skin, made to appear more ivory by her thick black hair, dark eyes, and perfect white teeth. We were opposites in nearly every respect but one. Like me, Alice was a bit of an outsider. Her intensely attractive, young parents weren't American. They had immigrated to New York from Syria. Of course, Alice shared one important thing in common with the other girls in our dorm: her parents were as wealthy as movie stars.

My first-ever Jewish friend, Alice was also the only rich friend I'd ever had. She hadn't known anyone like me before, having spent her entire life in New York, first in Brooklyn, and later in the predominantly Jewish town of Great Neck, Long Island. Outside of Israel, Great Neck probably had more Jewish delis and stores selling kosher products than any place in the world.

Alice's house overlooked the water in the wealthiest section of Great Neck, King's Point. The refrigerator and huge freezer were packed with food, bagels, gallon buckets of ice cream, cheesecake, and chicken salad. My mother shopped at the ill-lit Air Force Base commissary, where prices were low and the selection limited. Alice's parents took us to Broadway shows and afterwards to small, intimate French restaurants, where we'd inevitably spot someone famous. One night, Alice's mother leaned across the table and whispered, "There's Robert Kennedy." It was the year before RFK was shot.

Best of all were the shopping trips. They started on Long Island, at Loehmann's. Alice and her mother moved around the discount designer clothes store as if they'd been hired by the manager to inventory the merchandise. Mostly, they were interested in what labels and styles were available at Loehmann's, and at what price. Alice's mother took notes in a spiral binder that fit snugly in her palm. The notebook was attached to a gold chain connected to her large black leather bag.

Alice's mother would suddenly announce that we were done, and we would drive into Manhattan. We shopped in stores I wouldn't have dared go into on my own—Saks Fifth Avenue, Bergdorf Goodman, and some small boutiques and shoe stores I didn't know the names of. If I hadn't been with Alice and her mom, the clerks and security guards would have assumed I was there to shoplift. Alice and her mother swept through those stores like a storm, lifted shoes, purses, skirts, blouses, and scarves in their path, and dropped them on the counter.

No matter how many items Alice and her mother picked up, we always walked out of those stores without a single bag or box. That's because Alice's mother asked to have all the shoes, skirts, dresses, scarves, and handbags sent home.

The following day, boxes of stuff arrived at the house.

Alice stepped out of her jeans and began to try things on. Her mother pulled out the little notebook and jotted down more notes. Atop the bed, rumpled skirts and blouses soon formed a messy little mountain. A smaller clump collected on a nearby chair. There were yeses and maybes and outright "no's," along with items that could be had at Loehmann's for less.

At the end of it all, Alice had most of her spring wardrobe set off to one side. The remaining clothes and boxes of shoes and bags were sent back to the stores.

Alice and I both wanted to be thin, but I had an easier time. Tennis and jumping jacks and not eating Hershey bars bought from the basement vending machine in the dorm helped me lose extra pounds. Alice, though, had trouble saying no to the foods she liked. In fact, Alice had a dirty little secret. She was a binge eater. After gorging, Alice found nifty little ways to give that food up.

Before I went home with Alice on vacation, I hadn't known there was such a thing as binge-eating. At my house, we never had enough enticing food to make me overeat. Alice's house, on the other hand, was a dieter's hell. Plus, Alice's style of eating ensured trouble, no matter what.

The downstairs freezer at the King's Point house was stuffed, with gallon cardboard containers of ice cream taking up much of the room. It looked like an ice-cream parlor in there, with so many containers and different flavors. My mother only bought one half-gallon of ice cream at a time, usually butter pecan or cherry vanilla, both flavors I didn't like. At Alice's house, they even had my favorite, mint chocolate chip.

Rather than take a scoop or two of ice cream from the bucket and drop it in a dish or onto a cone, Alice brought a tablespoon to the ice cream. Watching her shovel ice cream straight from the gallon bucket into her mouth, I found myself wondering if she would ever stop. But it wasn't only ice cream. Late one night, while her parents were asleep upstairs, Alice consumed a bagel with cream cheese and lox, leftover cold potato pancakes and chicken salad from a pastel-colored Tupperware container. After that, she slid a cold roast chicken leg and thigh into her mouth, chased with a fat kosher dill pickle.

I never saw Alice throw up, but she assured me that she did. Her other remedy for all that gorging was Ex-Lax.

By my third year at AU, there wasn't enough money for me to stay in school, so I dropped out. I got a job selling car insurance downtown. The pretense I'd managed to keep up at AU, that I was just like Alice and my other rich Jewish friends, was gone. I quickly lost touch with everyone.

After Alice, I never had another best friend. There were a string of boyfriends and lots of girlfriends who came and went, and a husband who has thankfully stayed. But that one special person, close as a sister minus the meanness, has never come back.

Maybe if I'd stayed in one place for any length of time, I might have made and kept a best friend for life. But after dropping out of college, I kept on moving, first to New Jersey, then back to D.C., and afterwards to New Mexico, then California before heading up to Washington, back down to California, finally to Portland, Oregon, and then back to California again. So, I can't be sure. All I know is that the empty place in my life where a best friend ought to be throbs with an aching I can't wish away.

Lately, I've started imagining how it would feel to sit with my best friend over coffee or lunch, the conversation flowing as easily as a dream. I remember then what I'm missing: the firm belief that this person will always be my friend, no matter what I do or say.

I can't help wondering if it's me or whether the world has changed. I start to assume this new friend I've met might be more than a casual acquaintance for an occasional cup of tea, and that she might call with a last-minute invitation or reveal a closely held secret. Then something shifts. Suddenly, my friend gets busy and has no free time. The distance stretches from days into weeks and months. The memory of our shared experiences and conversation fades, like red does when left too long in the sun. The next time I get together with my friend, it's not the same. It's as if someone has burst in and snatched my potential best friend away.

Maybe it's old-fashioned of me to want a best friend to hang out with, rather than an occasional email or text from someone I only vaguely know. The close relationship I ache for might no longer exist. Perhaps I should have grown out of this longing before now, filling my need for a best friend with a husband and children.

Like all the best friends I once had in my life, my childhood glass horse collection is long gone. But I still collect dolls. The best are handmade and one of a kind. My favorite, the closest thing I have to a best friend now, is a doll I call Ms. Pookie.

Ms. Pookie has blond hair, large round eyes, and her

own mind. She reminds me of myself when I was young. I admit I've given Ms. Pookie some traits I'd prefer not to own. Ms. Pookie is selfish and stubborn and doesn't get along with any of my other dolls.

Ms. Pookie doesn't have a single pal, except for me. Like her owner, Ms. Pookie spends a lot of time alone.

17

DIFFERENT

LAURA AUSTIN

"I don't have any friends! Nobody likes me," my daughter keens, collapsing onto my bed.

Her anguish reanimates my nine-year-old self. In my mind, I'm a third-grader at our local Catholic elementary school, and we aren't allowed to wear pants, except on Fridays. Even then, no jeans are allowed. So, my mom sews me mostly dresses.

My mother worked her way through college as a seamstress in the drama department of her university. She makes all my clothes for me now, and today, we are working on a whole new wardrobe. I'm ecstatic to have a collection of unique, brand-new dresses made just for me. Mama lets me select the fabrics and the patterns, and we decide to make five dresses, just like the ones Laura, Mary, and Carrie wore in the Little House on the Prairie books. Kneeling on the floor in our den, Mama begins teaching me how to pin the fragile paper patterns to the fabric. I feel special and loved, especially knowing that my baby sister is Not Allowed. This is just for the two of us.

"Nobody likes me," I tell her, rolling onto my back next to the meticulously pinned fabric.

"I like you," she replies. Then she shows me how to cut carefully around the pattern without cutting into it. I chew on my hair, and I am thoughtful.

Later, I sit at my desk, holding a purple Crayola marker. Mama had bought me a "just because" present when we were out buying fabric. I open the mint green journal with a unicorn on the cover and begin to write. "Mondays—red dress," I scrawl. "Tuesdays—brown dress with pink flowers." In my immature grip, I write the details of the clothes I plan to wear to school that week.

Mama is an English professor and a firm believer in the importance of reading every night. At bedtime, after getting my pajamas on, I crawl under her warm cotton quilts and nestle into her loving softness. She reads to me; her voice and Laura Ingalls Wilder cast a spell over me. I am pulled toward sleep, toward dreaming of friendship and family in another place and time. When she finishes each chapter, I rouse enough to beg for "just one more chapter," but she sends me off to my own bed.

At school on Monday, I wear my precious red prairie dress, which my mother and I designed and made together. "Do you like my dress?" I ask Becky, who sits next to me. I stretch out the long skirt to show her. "You're so weird," Becky replies. I feel ashamed without knowing why. I turn back to my workbook. I can see that I am different from the twelve other girls in my class but don't understand the how or the why.

At recess, the other girls run away from me, giggling together. Becky's hair, styled in perfect spiral curls, bounces as she runs off. I suddenly think of Nellie Oleson, the mean girl who Laura Ingalls encounters in On the Banks of Plum Creek. "Who needs friends like that?" I think, and I go to sit at the picnic table. Fighting off hot tears, I put my head on my arms. "I don't need friends who are petty or cruel when I have Laura Ingalls, Anne of Green Gables, and Rebecca of Sunnybrook Farm. My friends all live in books, but they'll never laugh at me." I am nine years old, but I understand that being lonely and being alone are not the same thing.

I come back to the present, to my miserable nine-year-old daughter. "Not everyone is going to like you," I softly tell her, "and that's ok. Not everyone is going to be your friend." I pause, struggling to find the words to not merely help her understand, but to salve the hurt we all experience at being excluded. I want to pull her to my chest, to wash away her tears and take away her sadness. "The important thing is that you learn to like yourself. I love you, and I think you are awesome. I want to be your friend."

This is not what she wants to hear. She shrieks and growls, kicking and pounding at my bed. Then she runs to her room, where she slams the door and shrieks again. Being a parent can be isolating and lonely, painfully so at times. It's been thirty years since I was a third-grader, but the pain of encountering the Nellie Oleson's and Becky's of the world lingers.

After a few minutes, I head into my daughter's room.

She's in league with a stuffed animal and a graphic novel. "Do you want a hug?" I ask.

"No," she replies without looking up.

"Ok. I'm here if you need me."

I step back into my room to phone my husband. "It's Thursday," I remind him. "I have moms' night out this week. You can still get home on time, right? And make sure to put the kids to bed."

Tonight is my one night a month reserved to spend with friends. Too often, I miss these Moms' Nights Out. But when I do go, I know I am with my tribe and we're all weirdos together. We rant and rave and talk about our kids and partners and life, love, and struggles. Then we all leave, feeling less alone.

Once, I believed that I was the only one who felt isolated, excluded, and alone. I filled my world with friends who lived in books and stories. Together, we went on adventures, solved mysteries, and traveled across galaxies. These "friends" took me to worlds where I could believe in myself. The whole weird and wonderful, kit-and-kaboodle of strengths and weaknesses makes people special. I learned to embrace an imperfect me in a flawed and unfair world. Literature taught me that weird was normal. When I learned how to be my own friend, I was also lucky enough to discover my fellow weirdos. And those folks? They've become my tribe, the friends that are there for me when life feels impossible.

Tonight, parenting feels insurmountable. I need my tribe. We sit at Starbucks, doing crafts and chatting for hours. Our struggles and triumphs bring us together. After the barista tells us that they're closing shop, I stand in the parking lot chatting with my friends, Vickie and Tara. We're all shivering in the cold before finally admitting that it's time to leave, hugging and heading off in separate directions.

At home, my children are (blessedly!) asleep in bed. I stroke my youngest child's head softly, the way my own mother once did when coming home late some evenings. My daughter smells of baby soap and lotion, and I think my heart might burst from loving her. I want to tell her, "It's okay to be different. It's okay to feel lonely. Be yourself; love yourself. I promise you'll find your people. The friends you want and need are out there—I promise."

I wish I could take away her frustration and pain, but like all of us, she will need to learn these lessons for herself, in her own way and time. In the meantime, I can offer her Calvin and Hobbes, The Chronicles of Narnia, and Harry Potter. There is more than one kind of friend, and many balms to soothe our hurts.

18

HOW LONG IS A MINUTE? 1954

LEE MELAHN

I didn't grow up in an age of playdates or in a zip code where themed birthday parties were the norm. On your birthday, if you lived in my neighborhood in Madison, Wisconsin, you got together for cake and milk and general mayhem with some neighbor kids and a few cousins close to your own age. Although it wasn't too unusual for a classmate to invite a few friends, it was unheard of for a classmate to invite an entire class to their birthday party. So, when I got the invitation to Billy's party, it was a big deal. It broke all the rules. First, he lived more than two blocks outside my neighborhood. Second, we weren't BFFs; we weren't even just friends. And third, we weren't on the same pee-wee baseball team; we weren't even playing the same sports if you know what I mean.

I was more likely to get an invitation to his little sister's party than his. I was the kid who had to make sure he didn't show up at school wearing any shade of yellow on queer

Thursdays. I had full confidence that this invitation was a result of some cock-eyed rule Billy's pseudo-progressive mom heard and thought she'd instigate before she fully thought it through.

"Billy, I think you need to invite everyone in your class if you want to invite any of them."

"Oh, Mom, do I have to?"

"You're going to have to invite everyone or no one at all."

Billy would have to invite me, or he was going to end up without a party. All he really wanted was to get his buddies Mickey and Donnie invited and any other boy that might bring a boy-approved present or weapon. I think his mother was by then in too deep to change her mind, so Billy handed out his invitations to everyone in our fourth-grade class. The boys got theirs accompanied by a punch in the arm. The girls and I had the invites slapped on our desks with a thump and a growl.

This was to be historic; a co-ed party was almost unheard of. We were all stoked for that coming Saturday afternoon. Billy's mom may have had some last-minute regrets, but at this point, she wasn't quite mean enough to prevent any of us "no counts" from entering the party.

For me, the party went downhill the minute I walked through Billy's front door. I heard Billy's mom whisper to one of the other parents, "Who does this one think he is?" a comment I'm sure had everything to do with my white dress shirt and bowtie. I mean who doesn't dress for a party?

The party fare included a typical sheet cake, vanilla ice cream, and cookies served on paper plates with plastic utensils. Billy's birthday fell within the school year, a month after the beginning of the second term. It meant it was winter in Wisconsin, so the party had to be held inside. The preferable birthday months were during the summer, when all the festivities could be held outside, far away from the Hummel figurines and reproduction colonial furniture. Our hostess, Billy's mom, and her party assistant, Billy's mother's younger sister, had come up with some organized games to help pass the time. The games were all the typical games of chance: pin the tail on the donkey, clothespins in a bottle, and pin your buddy to the floor. It was a vain attempt at trying to divert the boys from turning any basement gadget into a gun and playing shoot-to-kill with all the squealing girls. At the very end of the party, after the gifts had been opened, and Billy's mom had decided it was time for everyone's parents to come and pick them up, his mom and her sister announced we were going to play one last game: "Can you guess how long a minute is?"

Before they started the game, they made all of us bundle up in our winter coats, assuming we would be less likely to re-instigate the chaos once we were tied and zipped into our snow gear. We were all bundled up so tightly that we could barely roll over on our own, much less get up and run around. They sat all of us down on the basement floor. The hostess held a stopwatch while her slightly dorky sister was given the task of keeping an eye on the contestants. I think both were pretty much at the end of their rope and very ready for the parents to show up and get us kids out of their hair.

"All right, children, we're going to play a game called, 'how long is a minute?' We have one prize left for the winner. Now, you all sit very still, and when I say go, you wait until you think a minute has gone by, then raise your hand. The winner will be the one closest to a minute."

At the mention of another prize, we all became a bit more focused. Unlike the politically correct parties of today, where everyone is a winner, in the fifties, we understood losing. Billy's mom was anxious to get this game underway before the crowd of kids got distracted and managed to get up and start rolling around like pinballs bouncing off all her department-store furniture. Whether it was the fear of losing control or exhausted anger I witnessed in her eyes, the look she gave us meant business. She punched the stopwatch with a jab of her index finger and yelled, "Begin."

Some kids had no idea what was going on. A few hands shot up after the first five seconds. I thought everyone knew the counting method, so I began to count to myself, "One-thousand one, one-thousand two, one-thousand three...." I was surprised that the hostess didn't get her sidekick to try to engage us in conversation to prevent any of us from using that cheating counting method. But the harried sister seemed so focused on spotting raised hands that she was oblivious to my internal counting. Many of the other kids had dropped out at around thirty seconds while I sat there counting away. The hostess and her helper noticed most of the other kids were now out of the running. Miraculously, Billy hadn't raised his hand yet, although I could see he was getting fidgety. Billy's mom seemed to be giving him some sort of furtive glance every so often with a hint of secret signals delivered with downcast eye movements every time he looked as if his hand was going to bolt up. As the contest boiled down to Billy and me, our hostess' eye movements became a tennis match between the two of us. Maybe it was the fact that her son didn't really want to invite me in the first place, or maybe she thought I had airs (my white shirt and bowtie, while all the other boys wore striped tees), or maybe she realized there was a chance the birthday boy wasn't going to win this one, and now she wanted him to win. She seemed to have a plan for him to win. I was too focused on counting to notice the extent of her icy disdain and realize that losing, at this point, might be preferable to winning.

"One-thousand fifty-eight, one-thousand fifty-nine, one-thousand sixty."

My hand shot up. I looked around. I was the only kid with his hand in the air, and I had hit the minute right on the head. There was no applause. There was no time for Billy to raise his hand. No one said congratulations or slapped me on the back. There was just this horrible scowl on the hostess' face and Billy whining that he should have won; it was his birthday. Billy's mom leaned over and told her helper to check my wrists for a hidden watch. They hauled me up to the front of the remaining group and made me take off my coat and empty my pockets to make sure I hadn't cheated, or at least cheated with some time-telling device. The birthday boy's tears turned to giggles at my humiliation, and the others soon joined in. Parents began to filter in, picking up their children. I never did get the prize. I never told my parents. But I went home knowing I was at least smarter than Billy's mother.

PART VII

WHAT WE SHARE

Friendship marks a life even more deeply than love. Love risks degenerating into obsession, friendship is never anything but sharing.

—Elie Wiesel

19

BOARD IN THE SUBURBS

CHRIS WIEWIORA

I kept my right foot planted on our driveway as I rolled the skateboard back and forth, feeling and hearing the slow rotation of steel ball bearings turning inside the wheels. Specks in the black sandpaper-like grip tape reflected the sunlight, and the grit scraped my sneaker. I heaved in the thick, humid air that kept my sweat from evaporating.

I was psyching myself, and I couldn't determine if I were psyching up or out. I was delaying gravity. I looked like I was supposed to ride, but I wasn't riding.

It wasn't even my board. My buddy Dylan had loaned me his board. I had biked home with it on my handlebars and then hid it in my closet. I'd been practicing rolling down the driveway since I came home from my new bus stop.

I didn't yet know the meaning of the words shape, flow, and pop. I would come to know those words as the feel of a board; the motion of arcing in crisscross lines on the ground like a surfer riding up and then looping—cutting back—on a wave's crest; and the pound of the tail and then lift of the nose into an ollie that raised the board magically above the ground.

I was still at the top of our driveway—Mom was out on errands and Dad had hours left at work—in the lull of the suburb's afternoon. I was considering riding into the street.

I took my right foot off the ground and placed it on the board's tail, careful not to set my weight on it and seesaw backwards. For a second, I stood still. Then, the board began to roll.

I was headed down to the street, but first, the gutter. I'd jumped off or run out and away from the board the other times I rode toward it. This time, I stayed on. I bent my knees and led with my shoulder.

The front wheels dipped into the gutter. I tipped forward, the board's nose dove, and then I was pitched off. My knee shredded along the asphalt.

Blood leaked down my leg. I wouldn't be able to hide the blood that would ooze through pants. I was marked, and I would have to show my parents what happened and then tell them how I wanted to do that forever.

On a sheet of Mom's stationery, I wrote:

I want to skateboard.

Then I added a comma and what I meant:

I want to skateboard, and you can't stop me.

I tore the sheet from the pad. The sheet underneath retained a ghost of my sentence. I tore that second sheet off the pad, too. I crumpled it together with the first sheet, and I threw them both away in my bedroom's trashcan.

I had taken the stationery from Mom's drawer by the telephone. I only used my desk in my room to work on freshman geometry homework. I didn't have any small pieces of paper to write important notes on.

I set the board on my lap and the stationery pad on top. I tapped a pen on the image of a panda printed on the bottom of the board. The panda looked like the logo from one of Mom's World Wildlife Fund posters—except this panda's eyes drooped. Also, instead of *WWF,* the skateboard company's name, *enjoi,* was written next to a turd behind the panda.

I needed to tell Mom about skateboarding. She would be the first one home. I didn't want to wear pants and cover up my scraped knee. I didn't want to practice rolling down the driveway only when my parents were gone. I didn't want to keep hiding the skateboard in my closet.

I tried again, explaining what would happen and why:
I am going to buy a skateboard. I want to ride. I like it.

I tore the sheet off the pad. I set the board against my bedroom's wall. I thought I might as well let it be seen.

I walked down the hallway from my side of the split-plan house to my parents' bedroom by the garage. On the way, I replaced the stationary pad by the phone. Then, I placed the note on Mom's pillow. I went back to my room to wait.

Soon, Mom came home and said, "Hello" to the house. I scrambled for my math book, so it looked like I was working on equations. Mom appeared around the corner of my bedroom door.

"I want you to wear a helmet," she said.

I looked up from my desk. It wasn't the argument I expected. I wanted to skate the way I wanted to skate.

"No," I said.

Mom stared at me. I glanced back at the geometric combinations of angles and sides like they were important. I felt Mom fill the doorframe.

"Think about it," Mom said.

I shook my head.

"I'll buy one for you."

"I won't wear it."

I felt Mom leave.

The next day, at our family computer, I printed out a list of reports on head injuries for boys playing high school sports. Football topped the list. Skateboarding was a footnote.

***

The last time I skated over to Dylan's, his mom pointed me to his room. I found him holed up. I noticed the *enjoi* board, that I had returned, sticking out of his closet while he was studying for engineering exams at his desk.

I was always skating by myself. I downloaded skate videos from the Internet. Issues of *Transworld*, *Slap*, and *Thrasher* filled the mailbox; I brought skateboarding to me.

I started buying skate gear for cheap off the other quitters. I didn't go back to Dylan's house for boards because I hoped one day he might roll again. Instead, I paid this one kid Francesco, who lived at the front of the neighborhood, twenty bucks for his scuffed-up *Toy Machine* board with a graphic featuring an orange Cyclops' unblinking red eye.

At home, I waved a hairdryer over the worn grip tape and then fit a razor blade between it and the board's wood. I stripped off the grip tape in pieces. Underneath, I discovered the wood was dyed green. And there was a graphic printed on top of the board, too. I left a gap in the new tape near the tail to show a cartoon-drawn yellow-horned devil with a black, spiky mohawk who said in a word bubble, "Grip it and rip it!"

I had scoped out several houses with pool-filter machines churning on the side of garages. I found crabgrass-clogged lawns and gnats that swirled out of the weedy shoots sprouting up higher than the deed restrictions' limit; junk mail that crammed boxes and flyers stacked on doormats. I ding-dong ditched those places and noted where nobody answered the doorbell.

I had narrowed it down to two houses, with their back-yards ending at a lake-size retention pond: one with an unlocked chain-link fence and the other, a shoulder-high wooden fence. Both were on the corners of intersecting roads. I would have several directions to scatter if someone called the cops.

The chain-link house had a kidney-shaped pool with a nice curved shallow end that sloped into a bowled deep end. I imagined pushing off in the shallow end by the stairs and swooping up in an arc over the light in the deep end to clack my wheels on the tiles. Maybe I could push myself to grind over the deathbox where the water filtered out to get cleaned in the pool system.

I walked around the back porch. Through the sliding glass door, I noticed a yellow light. I curled my fingers around the door clasp like grabbing the edge of my board during an air. I pulled, and the door slid along its track.

Just inside, a single bulb shone from a lamp without a shade. The thermostat was set at 79 degrees, probably to cut the humidity, but speckled black dots of mold covered the carpet. A stale smell hung in the air. I went back outside to breathe.

The wooden-fenced house had a square pool with a plungingly deep deep-end. I would have to deal with skating several feet of vertical cement after draining the entire thing. If I rode up its walls, I would be parallel, and a dozen feet from the flat bottom.

When I climbed into the backyard, I felt a presence like someone squatted there. The dried scrub grass was short. I wasn't sure if it had been cut. By the pool, several dusty, unbroken beer bottles sat next to a sagging deck chair. Under the porch, ashes swirled when I lifted the lid of a grill.

I chose to drain the kidney pool because it felt safer. One night, I rode over there in the dark. I unraveled a coil of garden hose and plunked one end in the pool's murky water and then spooled the hose's length over the deck, across the lawn, threaded it through the chain-link, and put the other end to my mouth. I sucked in through my mouth and breathed out through my nose. I pulled the water out of the pool through the hose. I could taste the empty rubber. I hacked when a mouthful of water siphoned out. I aimed the hose out to the retention pond camouflaging the hose's copper end with brush, so it just looked like a swampy spot.

My wheels held to the ground bumping over the pebbles and crushed seashells mixed in with the asphalt. I stomped my back foot down as I flicked the board by pushing out with my front foot out at the same time. The board clicked against the ground, spun a half-rotation clockwise below me. I pulled up my legs and then caught the board with my feet. I loved doing pop shuv-its with the crack, swirl, catch that quickly traded the nose from the front with the tail in the back of the board.

I carved around the corner, away from our street, off to check on the kidney pool. On the small stretch, I did a 180 and then quick shuv-it, no pop, just to set my board back up. I was riding fakie, so I 180-ed again to ride in my regular stance onto the main street.

I heard the clink of metal on metal and then the slap and clip of urethane landing. "Whoops" came from a lanky kid with exaggeratedly long legs that sloppily careened with his board while his arms swung. I couldn't figure if he were grasping the air for balance or pumping his arms in joy. His smile got me stoked.

I saw a sheet of particleboard, not even plywood, hauled up on top of a green plastic recycling bin set next to a rail in a house's driveway. This kid had been rolling up, grinding across, and then hopping off. The metal on metal sound must have been from a 50-50 grind.

It was janky do-it-yourself-itude. I knew exactly how that felt, to make something happen with what you have, like finding a backyard pool to skate.

I figured the pool would still be there as I showed off to this kid skateboarding in my neighborhood. I started stretching my foot as far forward on the ground as possible and then pulled my board along and pushed fast, faster. I set my foot on my tail and tilted back, lifting my front truck off the road and balancing a manual in front of the kid's driveway with my back to him.

I set the front wheels back on the ground and pushed off again. I wanted to snap and grab my board on the wedge-like driveway a few houses down. As I pushed to pick up speed again, I figured if I made the trick, I would introduce myself, but if I bailed, then I'd pick up my board and skate off to the draining pool.

I rode up the driveway and popped an ollie, up, up. My trailing hand grabbed the side of the board in front of me between my legs. My thumb caught the grip tape, and my fingers curled underneath on the board's laminated bottom. I floated and turned in an arc.

I released the board, and my wheels landed. So, I rolled across the street to the kid.

He introduced himself as Adam and said, "That was rad, man."

"Thanks." I nodded my head. "This is kinda cool, too." I pointed to his ramp-to-rail setup.

"Wanna try?" Adam asked.

We tried each other's tricks: grinds and airs. It was like a demo: showing off and having fun just sessioning. I skated with Adam until the streetlights flickered on.

A few weeks later, when I remembered to check, the kidney house's chain-link was padlocked, the hose gone, and the pool refilled. I thought about going back at night with bolt cutters and renting a diesel pump, but I was skating every afternoon with Adam. I could already boardslide—that perpendicular *shush* sound as the middle of the board's wood skimmed across the metal railing was thrilling—and Adam could launch up and tap his fingers to his board in a quick grab.

Dad squeegeed the condensation off his car's windshield. He wore clip-on shades over his glasses, even though the sun's orange ball of fire barely lifted over the horizon at the end of the street. I walked down our driveway, and my cargo shorts swished above my Vans. When I opened the passenger door, jazz hummed on the radio with double bass and swishes from the brush-sticks on drum skins, with cymbals occasionally tinkling. We always listened to public radio on the way to my high school because we rarely talked.

Dad shook his wrist, and droplets of water flicked from the squeegee. He set his squeegee underneath his seat and sat down. Dad started the car but left it in park.

"You know," Dad said, "You need to write your application essay?"

I pinched the bridge of my nose and nodded.

Dad drove me half-an-hour to school every day before driving back south another twenty minutes to his work. The bus stop was only one mile away. I walked home every after-noon. I never asked Dad to drive me to school; he just did.

As we started to roll down the road, I stared out the window at spots I skated on our street: The bricked driveway my wheels clicked over. The border of hedges I carved as I imagined their green semi-circle to be a wave. The manhole cover I ollied. The curb I scraped with my trucks as I took the corner against traffic.

Dad drove out of the neighborhood. At the bus stop for another high school for kids zoned in our neighborhood, I lifted my chin to Adam, and he waved.

The land opened wide to fenced-in pastures. I imagined crooked grinding from one railing over the post and then sliding and rolling to the next along the entire row parallel Dad's car. I stared out my window, framing the landscape, and put myself on it, riding it, like playing *Tony Hawk Pro Skater* and finding impossibly connected lines.

I projected myself skating at a strip mall: I would power-slide down the parking lot, slappy the curb, and then roll up the wheelchair-accessible ramp to launch into a wallride on the side of the building. My eyes connected the line, and my feet on the floor of the car twitched.

A fart-like honk of a saxophone from the radio pulled me back into my body. I wished I had that bag of tricks and that release from physics to float all over the constructed world. I glanced ahead on the road filmed with rainbow slicks of oil dripped from cars like ours following a track to school and then jobs. I turned back to look out my window.

My wheels clacked over the spaces between the orange-stained sidewalk blocks. I pushed along the zigzag next to the curving road. I listened for Adam's wheels echoing behind me.

As I picked up speed, I bent down and reached out my hand to brush the spongy Saint Augustine grass. Sprinklers clicked in yards, and misty well water stunk.

We had skated almost two miles out of the neighborhood. We passed the red-sided silver- roofed open-aired elementary school. We skated where a few years before, there had been only cattle that chomped on scrub brush and slept under the shadow of an occasional oak draped with the curly seaweed-green of Spanish moss. This new neighborhood was called The Preserve. An egret with its golden eye staring out was stamped on an emblem of both sides of the front gate.

A cluster of pines bordered a retention pond. When I spotted a low, gray rectangle of thin wall supported with arm-thick steel pipes rising out of its edge, I stepped off and scooped up my board. I walked through a mound of bark mulch piled around squat palms. The landscape sunk toward the pond and the gray walls.

Two brownish wedges faced each other with a straight flat bottom between them. Trails of parallel lines curved and arced and traced on the surface. I made the marks with my skateboard's wheels when I first discovered the drainage ditches.

I dropped my board at the top of the bank and shoved off. My wheels dipped over the angled transition to the flat bottom. I pushed one, two, three quick times. I set my foot on the tail and carved up to the lip of the bank, which jutted out and where the sandy soil had washed out an edge. I locked my back truck, and Smith grinded. Metal crushed rock. Speckles of aluminum flaked off.

I shifted my weight off my back truck and unhooked from the lip, turning back into the bank. I skated to the other side. I stepped off my front foot, my back foot snapping the board's tail to the ground and then lifted up and turned, doing a no-comply. I looked like a stereotypical plastic flamingo in a retiree's lawn, except that I spun and then stomped back onto my board and continued my line.

I crossed the middle of the flat bottom. I leaned forward with my weight to pump the board to keep momentum. My wheels etched a figure eight onto the concrete. I rode up the angle, bent down to grab the edge of my board, took my front foot off the board, and pushed off the ground and pulled up into a boneless.

My right foot rose, and my left foot lifted. I floated. My left foot returned to my board. Then, I landed with my wheels spinning and rode up the other side to Adam. He gave me a high-five as I heaved in the dusty air.

My sweaty T-shirt felt shellacked to my back. After skating, I grabbed the bottom and tugged up. The shirt made a wet smack when it landed at the bottom of the plastic laundry bin in my room.

I noticed a piece of paper on my desk. Dad must have printed the University of Central Florida's application essay questions. Question four was circled: *What qualities or unique characteristics do you possess that will allow you to contribute to the UCF community?*

I knew I needed to write an essay for my college application there. Everything else was done. I sat at my desk and took out a pencil.

I set my middle finger on the tip and my pointer finger on the middle of the pencil. I used the tip as a tail. I popped a mini-ollie up and onto the edge of my A/P American History book and slid the pencil along the hardcover's edge. I flicked the pencil off, spinning it around, and then caught it with my fingers to land on the desk.

I looked at the question again. I only had to fill one page. That wasn't too much. The only thing I had honed for years had been skateboarding. It hadn't just been a physical activity. It was natural history: surfers evolved out of the waves and carved up onto the asphalt and over the concrete landscape. It was physics: establishing and breaking rules. It was law: freedom and happiness by trespassing and destruction of property. It was life: I woke up staring at the Popsicle shape of my board leaning against my wall and thought about riding through each class period where I used my pencil for finger skating, just like at my desk. At home, I skated until dinner and sometimes went back out again in the evening. At night, my legs shifted under the sheets with dreams of landing tricks.

I remembered a video I watched sometimes before I sessioned called *Modus Operandi*. One skater, Marc Johnson, had an interview at the beginning of his part. Over the clip of him grinding on a desk dumped in an alley, he said something about the process, how he did it.

I grabbed the question sheet and took it to the family computer. I booted up the PC. I put on a fresh shirt. I knew I'd want to skate afterward.

I opened up the video I had downloaded. I clicked forward and found Marc's part. His head was shaved bald and he spoke with a coastal vibe:

"The craziest thing about skateboarding is you say, 'What if I could do this, you know? I think I could probably do this.' And you can do it. You can take something that was pure thought, and you can make it a reality."

I leaned back in the chair. I scribbled about how I could bring creativity to UCF. Then I clicked back on the video. I wrote Marc's final sentence down about making a thought a reality, like wanting to go to school and then going to school. I had filled up the entire page.

I knew that what Marc said applied to more than my college essay; it also applied to how I had been trying to land a full-Cab. On the street, I would roll backwards and wind up to turn, but then make a 180, and maybe my wheels would screech a bit more of a turn on the ground. I would be facing perpendicular to where I had been going. I couldn't get myself to fully rotate and return to the same position.

I watched a full-Cab video online in slow-mo. I noted how the skater's shoulders directed him. If I could turn my shoulder, then my body, legs, and board would follow. I grabbed my board and headed outside.

I rolled down the driveway, hopped the gutter, and then started pushing backwards. I set my foot on the nose. I crouched down, ready to spring. I snapped an ollie and turned 180, but then kept my shoulders twisting, and my board followed around full circle. I landed and continued to roll.

"Board in the Suburbs" first appeared on *Atticus Review*'s "More Than Sports Talk" and was anthologized in *Best American Sports Writing 2016*.

20

A BIT OF MAGIC

TAK ERZINGER

I used to think the only miracles that take place in the forest happened in fairy tales. But last year, I experienced a miracle between its trees. My psychologist told me I needed to step outside.

So, like Snow White, I found myself fleeing into the woods, but this time, not from an evil queen but rather an illness, a mental illness. PTSD had brought me down a year before. The psychologist had meant I needed to place myself around people, but I had become afraid of people. I had been hurt so much by them that I wasn't sure if I could trust again.

This sunny, late February day, I walked briskly uphill toward the forest. Instead of seeking people, I scurried to nature. I scoured naked branches for a rare plant I had spotted the previous week. It's one of the first pre-spring bushes to open its flowers, and when it does—it's a burst of much-needed color after that long stretch of January and

February. Much to my delight, I found it, and it had already begun to bloom. As I drew closer to admire the plant, a voice startled me, "Do you know what you're looking at?"

I hesitated because, at first, I couldn't see where the voice was coming from—then I spotted a petite elderly woman on the edge of the path behind me. "Yes, it's Daphne-mezereum."

"Very good!" the old woman replied. "Now, how on earth do you know that?"

By now, she had cornered me between the bush and the path. I noticed thick tufts of bridal white, short hair sticking out from under her hat. She had icy blue eyes with a youthful, even mischievous flicker to them. For a second, I wondered if I did not imagine the whole scenario.

She repeated, "Well, how?"

I shrugged my shoulders shyly, "My husband taught me about this plant; he's a gardener and runs a company."

She moved into my personal space "Well, how about that! Mine too! Or, well, he was; I'm a widow now. Are you walking up the hill?"

I hesitated a bit and then yielded to her happy familiarity. "Yes."

She replied, "Good, I'll walk with you a spell," and with that, she grabbed my arm.

I discovered that her name was Rosemary, and like myself, she was a foreigner in this Alpine country and had also married a Swiss. She asked me, "What are you doing out here during the day, in the middle of the forest?" I explained to her that I came out walking here almost every day, and she asked me if I had a job. Here I was, in the heart of the forest, spilling the beans to a total stranger, but somehow, being in a natural setting, I felt more at ease. I told her that I had experienced a mental breakdown the year before, and she didn't even bat a judgmental eyelash. She kept her arm linked in mine as if she had known me all her life, or as if I were her granddaughter. As we reached the top of the hill, she turned to me and declared, "This is where I turn around." Then she reached out her hands, grabbing both of mine, and said, "Be patient with yourself. It was a pleasure to talk to you. See you tomorrow." Before I could process the meeting, she had turned into the bend on the path and disappeared out of sight. I was so taken aback by the encounter that I had forgotten to say that I had appointments the next day and might not see her.

Several days passed by before I could get out and go walking again, and I was wondering if my unusual encounter with Rosemary had perhaps been a one-time incident. As I ascended the hill where the Daphne-mezereum now bloomed fully, I felt my stomach tighten because I realized I was alone. My disappointment lifted when I heard a rustling at the edge of the route. There she was! Rosemary bent down to clear sticks away from a wooden shelter with a worn bench. I felt my spirit lift at the sight of her. She called me over to her as if we had known each other our whole lives. I asked, "What are you doing?"

She said, "This spot of land is mine; great view, don't you think?" I could only nod in agreement.

After she finished clearing away the branches, she called me over to take a load off and share the view with her. That afternoon, I discovered she was Austrian and that she and her village had suffered greatly post-WWII at the hands of the Russians. She and her two sisters had been teenagers when they witnessed and experienced atrocities from both Allied and Axis powers.

After sharing her tales of trauma with me, she asked me directly but not without kindness what had caused my suffering and how it was triggered. As I explained my story to her, I never once felt judged or made to feel that my problems were insignificant or that she made light of them. For a year, Rosemary and I met up at that bend in the trail at the edge of the forest, sharing the fresh air and stories about our lives. Her company, her acceptance, her honesty, her ear, her story, and her friendship built in me the beginning of some social confidence.

There, surrounded by the solitude of nature, a most unexpected place to meet people, I had found a kindred-spirit as old as my grandmother, who had recently passed away. On that particular path in the woods, I found a gentle and accepting friend. Her companionship eased my anxiety about merging with the world again and reaching out to make new friends. Just like in a fairy tale, I found a bit of magic in the woods and was blessed by this unexpected miracle of friendship.

21

AND THEN THERE WERE THREE

MYLES HOPPER

August 28, 2014. "Will you write about me when I'm gone? Like you did about Aaron?" Mickey asked this near the end of our phone call.

He had read my story about our mutual friend of more than sixty years who had died two years earlier of multiple cancers. He knew that I had traveled to see Aaron and had kissed him on his forehead to say farewell.

"Of course, I'll write about you. But it won't have to happen any time soon, Mickey. You'll be home in a few days, and we can plan my visit to you."

Summer 1971. When Mickey and I were nearing thirty, we each purchased a Volkswagen van and converted them to campers. After wandering separate paths within North America, I stopped on the Atlantic Coast of Newfoundland.

He stopped five thousand miles away, on the Pacific coast of British Columbia.

It was there that he met a woman who had stopped her own wandering; together, they built a cedar and stone home where they lived for sixteen years and became a family with three children. Then, they moved to Los Angeles. During the next twenty years, they pursued various professional opportunities, the children grew into young adults, and Mickey and his wife divorced. In 2006, he returned, alone, to Lund, British Columbia, the place he loved the most. He had sold his original cedar and stone home and now began to live in various temporary housing on the remaining acres of his property.

Fall 2012. Six years had passed since his return, and Mickey began to build a new home he designed to sit on a bluff with a spectacular western view. In an email, he wrote, "I'm not going anywhere else, Hops (his nickname for me). This is the last house."

He was approaching seventy and was content with growing old. By the following year, everything changed. When I think of his emails from the years two thousand twelve to fourteen, it's like thumbing the pages of a notepad to create a moving picture, images that flash quickly in succession. Some flashes are most prominent.

- Stage 3 Barrett's Esophagus. Bought a food processor.
- Esophageal cancer. It hasn't spread.
- Radiation today. First chemo tomorrow. The oncologist expects a cure.

•Split two rounds of firewood. Felt good. Enjoyed the warmth.

•Most likely have bone cancer. I will know more next week.

•$250 on drugs to counteract chemotherapy nausea, vomiting, bleeding eyeballs, toes falling off, damage to my spermatozoa!

•New watercolor to communicate my place in an ever-evolving-never-ending Cosmos.

•Completed 12 weeks of chemotherapy. I will do another three weeks.

•Esophageal cancer metastasized to the computer. It died. Actually, I think it was another condition having to do with Photoshop.

•Oncologist said cancer in bones won't kill me. Said I'll die from another cancer invading a more vital part of me.

•Will pay your flight from Milwaukee to Vancouver: $500-$600.

July 8, 2014. I called him a few days after reading this email about the cost of the flight to Vancouver. We spent a few moments on when I might travel to Lund, and then talked in depth about his artwork, something we had done many times for more than sixty years. This time, the canvas of our conversation was his cancer. Though both of us seemed to understand it was terminal, neither of us openly acknowledged it.

While we talked, I thumbed another of those notepads.

• Skilled drawings by a ten-year-old.

• Early, watercolor self-portrait, with distorted reflection in the bell of a trumpet.

• Pencil portraits of homeless men.

• Oil painting of Indian women begging for money.

• Print of multicolored koi in water shimmering with reflections of sunlight.

The flickering images halted at a watercolor of a 1940s automobile being absorbed, rusting, into the earth of the British Columbia rainforest, and shrouded by branches and vines that would never lose their grip. A foreboding, prophetic painting.

July 16, 2014. His next email: "Imagine the Cosmos, and two giant galaxies each with the mass of hundreds of millions of suns, caressing each other. This might be my last painting."

Time, the poet's "winged chariot," did fly. In less than a month, it carried Mickey to the Powell River Hospital, where and when this story began: "Will you write about me when I'm gone?" And my answer was, "But it won't have to happen any time soon."

His body shut down, piece by piece. A scratch on his calf had become infected and wouldn't heal. The surrounding dead and blackened skin had to be ablated more than once. The hint of wheezing that I first noticed a few weeks earlier during our phone calls to each other had become labored breathing.

He said, once again, that he wanted me to come there.

"Of course, I'll be there. But I need to ask— have they scanned your lungs?"

"They did yesterday. I'll know the results tomorrow."

Two days later, he was discharged with medication to control the pain from his new combination of cancers: bone and lung.

September 4, 2014. During one of our many subsequent phone conversations, he said he was in bed all the time and exhausted.

"The home health visitors rub lotion on my legs and back and make sure I have plenty of fluids to drink."

"I can do that for you."

"Sure, you can," he said, pleased, as I was, by the very idea. "They also bring me groceries."

"I'll go to Lund and get everything you want, and if you can't read, I'll read to you."

"That's perfect. I'll really enjoy that. I think I don't have much hair...can't see myself or turn to see behind me... ocean and mountains."

I felt beyond angry at his caregivers. Why couldn't they do what I wasn't there to do? He had oriented his home on a bluff with an incomparable view of the rainforest sloping toward the sound and the mountains on the islands to the west. I refrained from the obvious, "Can't they rotate your bed?" I settled for, "Can they hang a mirror or stand it on the floor in front of you? Never mind, Mickey; I'll do the mirror." The vista would be reduced to a mere reflection of its magnificence.

When I told him that I'd call him back that afternoon with my travel plans, I was thinking about how many times I said I would be there and how many times I failed. The trip seemed overwhelming: Milwaukee to Vancouver. Two airplanes. And terminals. Commuter flight to Powell River. Taxi to Lund, where the only coastal road heading north terminates. Expires.

The next afternoon, Friday, I called to say I would be there Monday.

"…Oh…Monday…Okay…" Mickey said, each word framed by deep inhales.

"I can get there tomorrow, Mickey. I'll call you later."

A friend who is a travel agent began to make the complex reservation for early the next morning. Certain that Mickey's sister was already in Lund or soon would be on her way from Los Angeles, I called her mobile phone in the late afternoon to avoid surprising her by my arrival.

"Are you in Lund?" I asked her.

"I'm going on Sunday. Since he died this afternoon, there's no hurry."

"Died? What do you mean, 'died'?"

"Died. You mean you didn't know?"

"No. Tell me he wasn't alone." I could barely speak the words.

"Four friends and neighbors held his hands and feet. He was unconscious, but they held him until he stopped breathing." Then, she said something I hadn't known, didn't want to hear, and won't forget. "When I think of him that last eight days or so, it's excruciatingly painful to have heard from one of his friends that the last night Michael was on his own before going to the hospital, he was sitting on the steps of his mobile home, alone, in the dark, weakly calling his beloved Jumper. 'Jumper. Jumper. Come, kitty cat. Jumper.'"

It took about an hour of thought before I decided not to travel to Lund. The three children and their mother had to resolve some private and contentious estate matters. Besides, Mickey had needed me when he still lived.

Following his death, I failed to keep the promise I had made to write about him. After several weeks of not writing a word, I sat with the members of a small group that met regularly in a church classroom to read aloud and discuss our writing. I listened to a woman in her eighties read about the still-painful loss of a precious childhood possession. As she spoke, I was transfixed by the old-fashioned school clock on the wall. Mindless of what was in the hearts of all of us who sat under it, each tick of the clock's second hand, each click forward of its minute hand, consumed bit by measurable bit of what was left to us. When the minute and hour hands met at twelve, the bells of the church began to toll, "Softly and tenderly, Jesus is calling, calling for you and me ... Come home! Come home! Ye who are weary, come home!"

A half-hour later, under a nearly cloudless sky, the sun was a warm kiss on my forehead. The kiss I hadn't given Mickey. The kiss he knew I had given Aaron the day before his own death. Trees that had been autumnal gold and red and orange were almost bare. I shuffled my feet through dry leaves, as children do, and created a path like the wake of a small boat in still waters. A quick breeze scattered the leaves and covered any sign that a living soul had passed by.

October 4, 2014. Yom Kippur, the Day of Atonement, a day of fasting, and asking forgiveness from God and humans for any transgressions…including broken promises. This is not a proper day for writing, but I try and fail. I walk into the garden and perfect weather for transplanting. The first hard frost is approaching, and glistening droplets of fine mist coat the plants, many still green. I work with my ungloved hands in the cold earth and mulch, and I am visited by a prayer, the one we sang last night at a Yom Kippur service. I don't consider the meaning of the words, but only how they sound in ancient Hebrew and the melody I have heard since birth:

Aleinu le'shabeiach la'adon hakol, lateit gedulah leyotzeir beresheet…

In the garden, I hum and sing that first line of the prayer, over and over. As I conduct this Yom Kippur service for a congregation of one, bells begin to toll from the direction of the church I had sat in only days earlier. It is noon. It is the hymn I had heard when sitting below the ticking school clock.

The Christian hymn and the Jewish prayer intertwine. Each becomes part of the other:

"Softly and tenderly, *Aleinu le'shabeiach la'adon hakol,* Come home! Come home!"

I work until it's time to clean the spade and the garden-er's knife, scarred from years of use but still straight and strong. I store the tools in the wooden shed, aged to silver grey. In the garage, sandals replace gardening shoes, but I don't disturb the earth clinging to their soles.

Inside the house, I begin to write the only way I can. I talk with my friend.

"Today is Yom Kippur, Mickey. I ask your forgiveness for my not being there to read to you, to rub lotion on your back and legs, and to bring you food. I hope that you drifted away amid a dream or, perhaps, the reality of a glorious voyage to what you imagined might be your place in an infinite cosmos, your final work of art."

Though I try, I can't write anything more.

April 22, 2018. "It's good to talk with you again, Mickey. Can you hear me? It's April now, and it must be lovely where you used to dwell. Every spring, I think about how you and I walked through the woods near your first home in Lund and gathered sorrel and fern to decorate the table for Passover and Easter dinner with your friends and family. This spring, I've been sustained by the love and support of my remaining friends and family after we learned there's an intruder in my body.

Three of us. First, it happened to Aaron, then you, and now, it's my turn—exactly for what, I don't know. I do know that if anyone writes about me, it won't have to happen any time soon. Time. Does that word still have any meaning for you? I remember how much time went by, and I never really answered what I understood was your question, the one I now ask of you: Where are you, dear friend, when I need you here?

This work was previously published in *My Father's Shadow: a memoir*, Orange Hat Publishing, March 2020.

22

SHOWING UP

ELAN BARNEHAMA

In September of 1969, the NY Mets were in second place, the Vietnam War was raging out of control, and Blind Faith released their self-titled album with a naked girl on the cover. And I was walking along 67th Ave, across Queens Boulevard, past 108th St, on my way to my first day at Forest Hills High School.

In history class, the teacher put me and this kid who also had those old-school, Coke-bottle-bottom glasses together in the front row. Henry was even younger than me. Being the youngest kid in a grade lost its appeal the moment girls decided they liked older guys. Henry was young for tenth grade because he did 7th, 8th, and 9th grades in a two-years, having tested into the Special Placement class. I pretty much just started kindergarten early and moved on from there. That made Henry officially smart, and it made me, well, just young.

When the Miracle Mets won the World Series, some of

the summer's optimism generated by the Apollo 11 moon landing and Woodstock returned. But then Lieutenant Calley was charged with killing 109 civilians at My Lai, the Chicago Eight went on trial for being annoying, and all around us, sides were being taken, lines were being drawn, and stakes were being raised. We stopped cutting our hair, started going to protests, and looked to rock and roll for meaning. When the baseball coach told Jimmy to cut his hair or get cut from the team, Jimmy proclaimed the situation a mockery and walked off.

I started hanging out at Sage schoolyard with Henry, Jimmy, Ritchie, Sam, and Freddy and others. Except Freddy never played ball at all. Freddy could talk, and Freddy could drive. He was the first one of us to get a car, even though he was not the first to get a license. Our energy was focused on consuming greater quantities and varieties of drugs, playing ball, and trying to get girls to like us. If we couldn't get them to like us, then we tried to get them to have sex with us. Equally unsuccessful ventures.

One evening, sweaty and tired from basketball at Sage, we walked by Tung Shing Chinese Restaurant when it was down by Queens Blvd and Yellowstone. The door past the main entrance was open, revealing a tiny bar and a table filled with complimentary appetizers. With no bartender in sight, we ducked inside and began stuffing ourselves. The bartender entered, and we ordered beers. Instead of laughing and tossing us out, he set us up with a row of drafts. Sure, the drinking age back then was 18. But we were 14 and 15.

In those pre-cellular, pre-digital, pre-social-anything

days, that tiny bar became our information hub. It's where we gathered before heading out, and Freddy could always tell you where each of us was. And on more than one occasion, he drove us home when walking and driving were at issue.

Nixon's draft lottery was introduced that December, and while we had a few years till our blue plastic lottery capsules would be drawn, the draft cast a shadow over everything. For the guys who "won' the lottery, their lives were changed instantly. It seemed that the more we learned in school, the more confusing the world looked. By then, Henry had figured out that formal education held little value for him. That's how smart he was. Me, well I knew that I wasn't smart enough to be smart without school.

Forest Hills had an open campus at the time — or at least we thought it did. The school was on triple session, and students were always coming and going, so Henry and I would head over to one of the delis on 108th St. for lunch. One day, we got into one of those deeply focused, intensely clear conversations that reveal the secrets of the universe, and nothing at all. It wasn't until we got back to school that we realized we had never even got our check. While laughing hysterically, I noticed I felt comfortable.

I'd always been an outsider, a first-generation, oddly-named, child of Holocaust-era parents who mixed three languages into most conversations with thick accents that I never heard. But none of that mattered as much as my atypical eyes. Their desire to focus one at a time meant that I couldn't look people in the eye. If I looked right at you, you would think I was looking past you. And I couldn't figure out a way to adjust my head to compensate. Think girls here. Think teachers. Think job interviews. But mostly, think girls. The doctor called the condition unusual but not uncommon. He was wrong. It made me unusual and uncommon. The only advantage it ever provided was when I was the quarterback at Sage. The defense had no idea where I was looking.

I'd gotten used to being an outsider and hanging out on the margins. But Jimmy and Henry and Sam and Ritchie and the others, they were not outsiders. They were amused by my eyes when it was funny—and did not hesitate to laugh—but mostly, they didn't give a shit. Jimmy maintained that our bond came from not having brothers. Jimmy and Henry didn't have brothers, but some of us did. What none of us had were brothers-in-arms, blood-brothers. Calling someone your brother was a thing back then, but for us, it was about family. All families begin with strangers, and we had formed our own. Together, triumphs were made sweeter, and defeats were softened.

And then I went to college at SUNY Binghamton while the rest of the guys either went to a city college or didn't go at all. After college—my college, Henry only took six credits—Henry and I rode my motorcycle across the country. The guys sent us off with a long night at Tung Shing, where someone thought it was amusing to sign Henry's name to the tab. After LA, Henry returned to the city and put those six credits to better use than most MBAs, and I returned to Binghamton, where Nisa was finishing her degree. When she was done, we headed to LA, then DC, finally ending up in Northampton, MA. I saw those guys less and less. They spread out a bit but stayed connected to NY and each other. My parents left Queens, and I started a family, and years passed without any contact.

And then my mother died, and I was in NY sitting Shiva. I was outside, taking a break with my boys, away from the well-meaning guests, when I heard Henry's booming voice call out, "It's a little Elan."

Henry was looking at my son Ezra, whom he had never seen. Didn't matter. Sam, who was a member of the same synagogue as my mom, got the Shiva call and thought Henry would want to know.

Henry got me invited to the next big gathering, and I saw everyone. There was no reason for them to take me back in. We had all changed. We had all become different people, but different still didn't matter. Nothing any of us had done had altered our DNA.

We held reunions at Tung Shing, which had moved west on Queens Boulevard. For a while, our families met there the day after Thanksgiving and then played ball at Sage. When Tung Shing closed their doors a few years ago, the pre-cross-country-motorcycle-ride tab remained unpaid.

If someone called a Boys' Night Out, I answered. If someone called an Emergency Boys' Night Out, or if something was an accusation rather than a proclamation, or a declaration, well, Jimmy ruled on those. If you weren't sure of the rules, you saw Jimmy. But first, you showed up.

And showing up turns out to be almost everything; it may not be the only thing, but it's a big thing. I reconnected with Jeff and Larry, and the group picked up some worthy stragglers like Steve, but the core remained, self-selected by showing up. There's been some stints in rehab, some surgeries, some arrests for heroin, one death by overdose, another after a short and one-sided battle with pancreatic cancer, and one was banished for betraying the trust. But Henry's limitless capacity for fun remains contagious. Jimmy continues to mock time by playing on two different softball teams at the Great Meadows—hair no longer an issue. And when Arye, my younger son, decided to leave college to work on his first startup, Henry was there to support him.

I spent much of the sixties and seventies looking for a revolution, and instead, I found friends. I really had no idea how rare that would turn out to be.

A version of this essay originally appeared in the HuffPost Life under the title "Can't Get Rid of These Guys."

PART VIII

STILL TOGETHER

Each friend represents a world in us, a world possibly not born until they arrive, and it is only by this meeting that a new world is born.

—Anais Nin

23

BRAIDED

JULIA ANNE MILLER

I am born of a family of women. The men leave, or they
die, or they're mean, or they drink. Sometimes they
wander in and out of our lives, but in general, they are
temporary.

Until recent years, my family had five generations of
women alive. As a young girl, I observed that women were
there when I needed them, that a woman is strong and
endures. Grandmothers, aunts, mothers, daughters, nieces,
sisters, granddaughters...our lives are as sturdy and inter-
woven as a thick rope.

I had three maternal grandfathers. My first grandfather
was a married man who had sex with a fifteen-year-old girl.
The first time I saw the one photograph we have of him,
taken in 1946, I was stunned. My youngest son looks like no
one else in our family, and there was his doppelgänger in
black and white, leaning against a car, long legs crossed in
front of him.

My second grandpa was a migrant worker named Henry, with dark blue eyes, a ready smile, and an easy manner. He sent big bags of Georgia pecans to us once a year, the words on the mailing label carefully copied like a child's designs because he couldn't read or write. He'd show up every so often to visit in his old, white camper, which was just a beat-up pickup truck with an enclosed bed that he called home. He'd stay a few days, then one morning, he'd just be gone.

My third grandpa was Choctaw. He joined the Army because jobs in rural Kentucky were scarce for all men, but especially for those with brown skin. I called him by his given name, John, at my mother's insistence. She thought of Henry as her father; so John couldn't be my grandpa. When I was five, John told me that he had almost shot me during the night while I was sleepwalking through his little green ranch house. He said it was real good to be having breakfast together instead and winked. I have a picture of us from that same visit. He's in uniform and kneeling on one knee. I'm sitting on the other knee in an entirely red cowgirl costume —dress, hat, boots, the whole deal. I look shy but pleased. He's grinning and looks large and protective. I didn't have much contact with John after that visit because he and my Grandmother Ada moved as the Army saw fit, but I did attend his funeral a few years ago, and I cried when my mother was handed the flag, folded up in a neat, tight triangle.

Henry and John were both good men—they left for work they couldn't find at home. But, as a child, my experience was that even good men leave.

My roots are along the Green River in cave country in

southern Kentucky. My family were mostly farmers, and some still are. My great-grandpa, who everyone called Pop, owned a few acres of land, a cow and a mule, hounds, and some chickens. There was also a rooster, who was equally mean and chased me whenever I tried to cut across the front of the house. That rooster terrified me, but Pop was scarier. When my sister and I would play in the woods, he'd hide in the bushes and growl like a wolf. At night, sitting on the front porch in the dark, he'd tell gory stories about wolves eating children. My great-gramma just rocked steadily, hugging us into her warm green beans and biscuit scent as we scooted close. Their house burned to the ground twice, and the only thing she saved was that old rocker. I have an image of her in my head, rocking in her chair out in the yard watching her meager belongings go up in flames, wondering how long they'd have to stay in the barn and cook over a fire. She was a practical and resourceful woman.

A few years ago, my sister Kas and I drove out to see the farm. We hadn't been there in many years. Another family lives there now, with lots of kids and dogs. The barn Pop built was still standing, and the house was, too. We were surprised to see it was pieced together, built one room at a time with available materials. The roof was patched in the same way, covered in practical solutions. It was nothing to notice when we were younger, but we're accustomed now to a world where things and people often match.

My great-gramma helped raise five girls from three generations on that farm. When times got hard, my family dropped their kids at Gramma's. When she was nineteen, my Grandmother Ada left her kids at the farm and moved to

Louisville to make money she could send home. Shortly thereafter, she succumbed to mental illness.

My great-aunt Gladys sold the farm after Pop died. She said it would be easier to take care of Gramma as she grew older if they lived closer to the textile factory where she worked. Aunt Gladys had lived her whole life on that farm with her parents, and she wanted indoor plumbing. She said a woman could only worry about snakes in the summer outhouse for so long, and fifty years was enough.

Aunt Gladys would show her tiny ranch house to everyone who visited, just like a realtor. She pointed out her electric oven, her bathtub, the garage where she parked her spotless car. The bathroom had matching pink towels, carpet, and soap. Her gold-plastic encased couch made crinkling sounds until reposers settled into place.

Gladys was a beautiful woman and just the tiniest bit vain. When I was a young woman, she would say, "You are so pretty. You take after me." And she meant it. Gladys enjoyed catching a man's eye, no matter his age. She would downright swoon when Kas took my tall and quiet brother-in-law, David, down to visit. He loves fine wine and gourmet cooking. He seems an unlikely match for Kas, even now, after thirty-five years. Kas is a farmer and has an entire acre fenced just for the dogs she rescues. She brings home horses from the Kentucky kill-lots too. And like Gramma, she has raised quite a few children, bringing them into her fold with all the other hurting creatures. But David doesn't say a thing in protest, probably because he works too far away to be bothered, traveling home for a few nights, then staying in town the others. Kas runs the farm with her daughters, breeding some animals and rescuing others.

Kas rescued me, too. When we were teenagers, mental illness got the best of our mother, and instead of wandering off as expected, our dad stayed home and drank. At the time, we were living in what's called an Urban Appalachian neighborhood in the northern part of Kentucky that's on the Ohio River. Kas and I both quit school, and she got a job driving a carriage for tourists around downtown Cincinnati, which is just on the other side of the river. I went to work in a fast-food restaurant and tried to get late shifts, so I could bring home left-over food.

Kas found us a small apartment in an old building where we camped for months. When it snowed the first time that winter, a tiny white pile collected on the floor, which was how we discovered the window frame had separated from the brick up top where we couldn't see it. It was so unexpected that Kas and I couldn't stop laughing. We stuck an old towel in the crack, like Gramma and Pop would, then took it out when it started to warm up outside.

About a year later, my daughter Ashley was born. I loved her father, but I was eighteen years old, and I knew how life worked. Sure enough, he left when she was six-weeks-old, disappearing into drugs and alcohol. Ash and I had lived in places where you keep the lights on at night and push heavy objects up against the doors and then in a shelter where it didn't snow inside. My mother-in-law Karen said she'd never seen anyone stretch a nickel so far. Karen and I have been friends for forty-one years. I gave up on my husband, but I kept his mother.

I also kept his second wife, Teresa, with whom he had four sons. I like to introduce Teresa as "my first ex-husband's second ex-wife" and watch people do the math in their heads.

Teresa helped me raise my daughter, and my daughter is perhaps the strongest woman I know. When one of her brothers was a teenager, he asked, "If you were in a bar fight, who would you want by your side?" Without pause, and in unison, everyone in the room said, "Ashley." Ash handles life like a preacher handles snakes: without fanfare and fear. When she gets bitten, she tends the wound; then, she moves on.

Alice Walker speaks of a "twin self," an inner self that is one's home. The "twin self" that my internal mirror reflects is that strong rope, the one made sturdy by all the women woven into it. If I removed any strand of that thick rope, I would unravel a part of myself. Each woman lives in the home inside me, where self and twin-self reflect each other. When I look in the twin mirrors, the images drop endlessly, one after another after another.

24

JUDGING GINNY

AMY LOU JENKINS

I refused to go with Ginny to the *Tie Me Up, Tie Me Down Tattoo and Body Piercing Parlor*. But she went anyway. She had a goddess image tattooed on the back of her neck. Then she had her nipples pierced. I can now see beyond the cringe-factor and imagine her offering her neck and her breasts for adornment as an act of directed ownership—a brave act, perhaps worthy of admiration. Still, this was her act of daring that was not and is not for me.

We *were* so much alike. We met at work, are both nurses, even have daughters about the same age. We vacationed, shopped, laughed with the girls at Friday-night game nights, screamed on roller coasters, picnicked with the kids at parks and lakes, developed presbyopia, and cared for each other's kids and each other during life stressors like getting divorced and going back to school.

My best friend, Ginny, got a divorce after sixteen years with a man who defined her as, "lucky to have me." She decided she was better to be rid of him and to stop living as his woman.

In most ways, her behavior made sense to me. She'd never been on her own. She married young and spent her youth serving her daughter and husband. We were both of the age when having it all meant doing it all—as if that were possible. We were Atwoods' edible women, to be assimilated into the family. Our very structure, our time, our strength, our sacrifice, our money invisibly held up the household, while we assumed secondary roles. Tidy front rooms and clean kitchens told one story, while darker corners hid secrets of full laundry baskets, piles of mail to attend stuffed in drawers, and vacuums with broken belts and full dirtbags idling in closets. Florescent chalk wrote to-do lists on the blackboard inside our eyelids, depriving us of peace. Together, we tried to make it look easy, to build the home for husband and family. The easier we made it look, the more accomplished we must be. Right? On parallel paths, we came to understand that we couldn't bear all with the men to whom we were yoked.

We carried the load of domesticity and professionalism and pretended we could do it all. But something always fell apart, until the marriages imploded and exploded.

Once free from her him, Ginny had the opportunity to perform the experiments usually associated with twenty-one-year-olds. She could consider her carnal self. And she did. I assumed the phase would pass because my carnal desires and actions came in waves, but they did not break as hard and fast as hers seemed to.

We went on a Caribbean cruise together. While I donned

snorkeling gear, she disrobed at a nude beach. While I picked at the midnight buffet, she sauntered by with a handsome Italian in a dress-white officer's uniform before disappearing for the rest of the evening. The next night, while I excused myself to use the bathroom off our main dining room, she exchanged phone numbers with a recently-divorced securities broker who drove a black BMW, owned two houses, and was saved from financial ruin by a prenuptial agreement. I was only in the bathroom for a few minutes, but it was enough time for her to decide he was a sloppy kisser.

I tried to convince myself that her crazy actions were a kind of normal delayed development because of her blunted youth. Then her daughter left for college. Ginny quit her job, sold her house, and joined a traveling nurses' organization, taking three to six-month assignments all over the country. She kept telling me how happy she was. I wanted to see that joy for myself. Wasn't what I saw as "empty sex" a misguided cry for love? How could she be happy?

I was thrilled when she took an assignment in our hometown for the summer.

"Oh, I'm so happy to see you." I even imagined this was a sign that she was settling down and ready to resume a more normal life—until she showed me the pictures.

"This is a wine and cheese-tasting party that I went to," she said, handing me the packet. A skinny man with a shiny watch and quite public private parts waved his cube of cheese at the camera. A round little couple, who covered their genitals with pendulous bellies, wore matching gray perms, posed with toothy grins, and faced the camera while leaning into each other. Another snapshot captured a full-frontal view of naked Ginny: a beautiful warm smile and a spiked haircut with blond streaks highlighting her face and hugging her neck. She was shaved, pierced, and proud.

I admit that I wanted to peep at these pictures. Part of me wanted the freedom and comfort they displayed. Most of me thought they should get dressed.

I was witness to my surprising lack of judgement about our relationship. I wanted her to be careful, but her shocking actions didn't make me love her any less. A part of me did want her to reign it in—to be more like me. But it just wasn't a deal-breaker.

"You do this sort of thing often?" I asked her. She pulled out pictures of nude pool parties in Houston, topless biking in Arizona, and naked movie-watching in a small Akron ranch-style home.

I told her that I thought this was a phase that she would grow out of.

"Ginny, you're over forty. My God, you wear bifocals. You've got to stop this crazy life."

My best friend Ginny laughed at me and showed me a picture of her walking on a beach near Boca Raton. Her bifocals hung conveniently through the hoop of one of her nipple rings.

Shortly before Ginny left for another assignment, a mutual friend appeared at my door. Looking rather grim, she asked me to join her in a Christian intervention. She planned that we would tell Ginny that we could not be her friends anymore. We would have to cut her out of our lives unless she changed. This mutual friend asked me to be Ginny's judge. Despite her scripture quoting (which omitted reference to Luke 6:37: "Judge not, and ye shall not be judged; condemn not, and ye shall not be condemned; forgive, and ye shall be forgiven"), and despite her praying, I refused to join her shunning. It didn't feel like love.

Sometime after this mutual friend began happily living, sans marriage, with a younger man, she softened her rules of disengagement, but she lost out on the closeness she had shared with Ginny.

During these decades of friendship, Ginny and I have changed, yet we don't try to change each other. She visited when I had surgery and tenderly washed my hair. We Facetimed while she needlepointed in the nude, and I wrapped birthday gifts. She's ridden waves of happiness and letdowns. Her lovers came and went until one came who stayed. We are both in long-term relationships. The ups and downs that she's experienced with many men, I've experienced with one man for more than twenty-five years in a monogamous relationship. Her long-term relationship abides upon different structures of agreement. We live many states apart but keep in regular contact. During our conversations, it never seems necessary to judge how clothed we are or are not or how or whom we sleep with. We talk about who we love, how we can serve others, if we are building meaning into our lives with our actions, what fun there is to be had, and how lucky we are to be growing older. Okay, we also complain about our weight and aches and pains.

Ginny is genuinely kind and fun. She serves others as a nurse, mom, volunteer, friend, and good person. She picks up litter. She'll crochet a blanket for your new baby. Sometimes, she visits sex clubs. If you waited on her in a restaurant or store, you'd feel better for the interaction. She's left a checkout line in the grocery store with a new recipe for zucchini pancakes. She tells the bagger he has great teeth. When the lady behind her in line compliments her pocket bag, Ginny gives her a discount coupon she happens to have in her purse for the boutique where she bought it. She will stop and pray with you if it seems that it would be a comfort to you, or not. She's quick to laugh and quick to love. I don't tell her to stop her crazy life anymore. If she does her best to stay safe, it really doesn't matter. None of her relationships are empty. If I tell her I need her, she will come. She has the same assurance. I think that these days, I could even accompany her to a piercing. All the lifestyle choices that could separate us, just don't.

THE WRITERS
BIOGRAPHIES

Leah Angstman is a historian, transplanted Michigander, and the editor-in-chief of *Alternating Current Press* and *The Coil* magazine. Her debut historical novel, *Out Front the Following Sea*, is forthcoming from Regal House Publishing in Spring 2022, and her writing can be found in *Publishers Weekly*, *Pacific Standard*, *Los Angeles Review of Books*, *The Nashville Review*, and elsewhere. You can find her at www. leahangstman.com and on social media as @leahangstman.

Laura Austin is an author and parent living in a cozy house north of Seattle with her spouse, six kids, and two dogs. Writing from her closet "office," Laura explores topics surrounding modern motherhood, education, and raising twice-exceptional children. When she isn't writing or wrangling kids, Laura enjoys reading, sewing, and gardening. She also adores dressing up in a corset and walking skirt —just because.

Elan Barnehama is the author of *Finding Bluefield*, a novel. His writing has appeared in *Drunk Monkeys, Rough Cut Press, Boston Accent, Jewish Fiction, Running Wild Press, HuffPost*, the *New York Journal of Books*, public radio, and elsewhere. Elan has taught college writing, worked with at-risk youth, had a gig as a radio news guy, and did a mediocre job as a short-order cook. He's a New Yorker by default and a Mets fan by geography.

Twitter: @elanbarnehama Web: elanbarnehama.com

Mara Buck writes, paints, and rants in a self-constructed hideaway in the Maine woods. She hopes to leave someday. Winner of The Raven Prize for non-fiction, The Scottish Arts Club Short Story Prize, two Moon Prizes for women's writing. Other recent first places include the F. Scott Fitzgerald Poetry Prize, The Binnacle International Prize. Awarded/short-listed by the Faulkner/Wisdom Society, Hackney Awards, Balticon, Confluence, and others, with work in numerous literary magazines and print anthologies.

Terri Elders, LCSW, a lifelong writer and editor, has contributed to over a hundred anthologies, including multiple editions of *Chicken Soup for the Soul*. She writes feature articles and travel pieces for regional, national, and international publications. After a quarter-century odyssey, including a decade overseas with the Peace Corps, she recently returned to her native California. She blogs at http://atouchoftarragon.blogspot.com/.

TAK Erzinger is an American/Swiss poet and artist with a Colombian background. Her poetry has been featured in *Bien Acompañada* from Cornell University, *The Muse* from McMaster University, *The Rising Phoenix Review* and more. Her debut poetry collection, entitled *Found: Between the Trees* was published by Grey Border Books, Canada 2019. Her second unpublished poetry manuscript was short-listed by Eyelands Book Awards. She lives in a Swiss valley with her husband and cats.

Natalie Esarey is a 23-year-old writer who is a passionate mental health advocate and a devoted mom to her dog, Gus. Her work has previously been featured on *Thought Catalog, Be A Light Collective*, and *The Mighty*.

Janet Garber earned an M.A. in English from the University of Rochester. Her essays have appeared in *NYT, WSJ, Working Mother, Chicken Soup for the Soul,* and elsewhere. *Dream Job, Wacky Adventures of an HR Manager*, her award-winning satiric novel, debuted in 2016. Janet lives on the outskirts of NYC with her hubby and two emotionally-challenged rescue cats. She's currently revising her second novel, *The French Lovers' Wife*. She welcomes visitors to http:// www. janetgarber.com.

Kathleen Gerard's writing has been widely published, anthologized, and broadcast on National Public Radio. She is the author of three novels: *In Transit, Cold Comfort,* and *The Thing Is*. Learn more at www.kathleengerard.blogspot.com.

Pat Hale's short fiction piece, *A Book of Matches*, was performed by the East Haddam Stage Company in its series Plays with Poetry. She is the author of the poetry collection, *Seeing Them with My Eyes Closed*, and the poetry chapbook, *Composition and Flight*. Her prize-winning work appears in many journals and anthologies. She lives in Connecticut, where she is proud to serve on the board of directors for the Riverwood Poetry Series.

Myles Hopper writes creative non-fiction and the occasional fiction story. He is a cultural anthropologist and attorney, has taught in universities in the United States and the Canadian province of Newfoundland and Labrador, and continues to consult with nonprofits in need of strategic planning. Publications include *My Father's Shadow: a memoir* (Orange Hat Publishing), and *Exodus Redux* (Hidden Timber Books.) He and his spouse have two adult children and live in Shorewood, Wisconsin. Website: myleshopper.com

Amy Lou Jenkins is the founder of Jack Walker Press. She holds an MFA from The Writing Seminars of Bennington, has taught writing at Carroll University, Milwaukee Area Tech College, and conferences and workshops, including NonfictioNow/Iowa Writers Workshop and Write by the Lake/University of Wisconsin, Madison. Her essays and stories have appeared in literary journals and anthologies, including *The Florida Review, Flint Hill review, Leopold Outlook, Sport Literate, Earth Island Journal, Consequence Magazine, The Maternal is Political, Journeys of Friendship, and Women on Writing*. She's the author of *Every Natural Fact; Five Seasons of Open-Air Parenting and more.* Her writing has been honored by US Book Award, Living Now Book Award, Ellis Henderson Outdoor Writing Award, and XJ Kennedy Award for Nonfiction and more. She pens a quarterly book review column for the Sierra Club. She writes for children under the name Lou Jenkins. She and her husband split their time between Wisconsin and Arkansas. Unless it's so cold it hurts, she'd rather be outside. Follow her at www. AmyLouJenkins.com.

Rich H. Kenney, Jr. is a former centerfielder who played on the East Braintree, Massachusetts, Little League All Star baseball team in 1963. He teaches courses in social work at Chadron State College in Nebraska. Recent works include poetry in *Plainsongs, Peregrine,* and *Social Work Today.*

Nancy London is one of the original authors of *Our Bodies, Ourselves,* as well as the author of *Hot Flashes, Warm Bottles: First-Time Mothers Over Forty.* She holds a master's degree in social work and was a hospice social worker for more than a decade. She currently lives in Santa Fe, NM where she has a grief counseling practice and leads writing workshops for women.

Steve Luebke teaches in the Department of English at the University of Wisconsin-River Falls. His poems have appeared in *The Lucid Stone, Mediphors, Poet magazine, The Wisconsin Poets' Calendar,* and *most recently, The Deronda Review.* His fiction has appeared in *The Writers of Wisconsin, Tribute to Orpheus, Rattlesnake Valley Sampler,* and *The Wisconsin English*

Journal. His novel, *Steps of the Sun*, was published by the Tri-Screen Connection in 2014 and may be found at web-e-books.com.

Lee Melahn commutes mid-coastally between his home in Madison, Wisconsin, and his apartment in NYC, where he writes his blog and works as an interior and furniture designer. He's been published in multiple shelter magazines for both his work and his opinions. His design work, along with his partner's, can be seen on their website: www.shavermelahn.com, and his stories, on their blog at www.pleasantlivinghome.blogspot.com.

Julia Anne Miller is a doctoral student of Humanities at Union Institute & University. She has taught undergraduate philosophy at the University of Cincinnati and Stony Brook University and lectured at Northern Kentucky University and the University of Kentucky. She has published poetry and creative nonfiction in a variety of literary journals, as well as the 2018 Jack Walker Press anthology *Corners: Voices on Change.* Most recently, her writing has focused on neuro-diversity and growing up in Kentucky.

Joanne Passet grew up on a sheep farm in northwest Ohio. Weekly visits to a nearby Carnegie Public Library fueled dreams of traveling the world and becoming a writer. Her latest book, *Indomitable: The Life of Barbara Grier*, was a finalist for a Lambda Literary Award in Biography. She resides in Bloomington, Indiana.

Adrienne Pine's creative nonfiction has been published in The *Write Place at the Write Time, Tale of Four Cities, The Yale Journal of Humanities in Medicine, Carte Blanche, Feminine Collective, Gravel, Shark Reef,* and other venues.

Betsy Robinson is a novelist, editor, and journalist. Her latest book of short stories and plays is *Girl Stories & Game Plays*. Her latest novel, *The Last Will & Testament of Zelda McFigg*, won Black Lawrence Press's 2013 Big Moose Prize and was published in September 2014. Her website is www.BetsyRobinson-writer.com.

Patty Somlo's books, *Hairway to Heaven Stories* (Cherry Castle Publishing), *The First to Disappear* (Spuyten Duyvil), and *Even When Trapped Behind Clouds: A Memoir of Quiet Grace* (WiDo Publishing), have been Finalists in the International Book, Best Book, National Indie Excellence, American Fiction, and Reader Views Literary Awards.

Chris Wiewiora is from Orlando, Florida, where he used to skateboard drainage ditches before graduating from the University of Central Florida. He earned an MFA in Creative Writing and Environment at Iowa State University. His nonfiction has been published in *Stymie: journal of sports & literature* and *Sport Literate*. Read more at www.chriswiewiora.com.

Tamra Wilson is a local columnist and a Road Scholar for the North Carolina Humanities Council, specializing in Southern literature and American history. Stories in her collection, *Dining with Robert Redford*, have appeared in *Epiphany, North Carolina Literary Review, The MacGuffin* and elsewhere. She is co-editor of *Idol Talk: Women Writers on the Teenage Infatuations That Changed Their Lives*, (McFarland, 2018). 'Dear Anne' was birthed within a sermon she delivered in 2014.

P.F. Witte is a New York City writer and photographer. She has won the Pat Parker Memorial Poetry Award and the Allen Ginsberg Poetry Series Award, among others. Her fiction, non-fiction, and photography work have appeared in the anthologies: *The Muse Strikes Back, Women on the Verge, The Writer's Place, The Literary Journal of the Kurt Vonnegut Museum and Library, The Family Narrative Project,* and the upcoming anthology *Rituals*.

THANK YOU

Thank you to all the writers who contributed to this volume by artfully sharing their life stories of friendship.

Thank you to each reader. Please support this book and every book you like by telling your friends and by posting your honest reviews at booksellers. Literature needs your support. Without you, literature dies.

Review this book easily by clicking on (Ad)
Friends at author.to/AmyLouJenkins.

ABOUT JACK WALKER PRESS

Jack Walker Press specializes in books for adults and children who believe that the best realities are Earth, life, and spirit. And the best virtual realities are books. We partner with you to celebrate just, verdant, thoughtful, and joyful living. Sign up to receive announcements, freebies, and submissions calls at Jack Walker Press Anthologies.

 facebook.com/JackWalkerPress.com